ON

AYN RAND

Allan Gotthelf
The College of New Jersey

Wadsworth
Thomson Learning.

Australia • Canada • Mexico • Singapore • Spain
United Kingdom • United States

Printed in the United States of America
   3 4 5 6 7 03 02 01 00

For permission to use material from this text, contact us:
Web: http://www.thomsonrights.com
Fax: 1-800-730-2215
Phone: 1-800-730-2214

For more information, contact:
Wadsworth/Thomson Learning, Inc.
10 Davis Drive
Belmont, CA 94002-3098
USA
http://www.wadsworth.com

ISBN: 0-534-57625-7

Preface

Ayn Rand is an American cultural phenomenon. Her books have sold over 20 million copies, have influenced countless lives, and have generated much intense admiration and some significant antagonism. Yet the philosophical system which her works express and on which they rest is insufficiently understood by many of her admirers and by most of her detractors; and she still gets little attention in academic philosophical journals and courses.

This book aims to help change that, by introducing its readers to Ayn Rand's philosophical thought. Within its compass it can only *introduce*, but it seeks to bring increased understanding to every reader who works through it, and it will point directions for further study.

The book is addressed primarily to the general reader and the undergraduate student of philosophy. With this audience in mind, the main exposition assumes no special philosophical background. It does assume a serious interest in learning about the philosophy that drives the works that have given Ayn Rand her enormous impact.

In writing this book, however, I have also had in mind the professional philosopher and the advanced student of philosophy. Though this book is inevitably introductory, it aims to expose interested philosophers to the range and significance, and some of the power of argument, of Ayn Rand's philosophical thought. It is high time that academic philosophers accept the responsibility of understanding, thoroughly and with full, professional expertise, this highly original thinker and the scope and content of her often groundbreaking thought. I hope to be of help toward that end.

In a book of this compass I cannot fully convey the subtlety of thesis and power of argument Ayn Rand's work incorporates. But in asides in the main text and especially in the endnotes, I have tried to add material that will assist readers in placing her thought relative to the thought of more familiar philosophical figures.

1

A word is in order about the background that I bring to this book. I first discovered Ayn Rand's works in 1961 as an 18-year-old undergraduate. About a year and a half later, I was fortunate to attend authorized lectures on her thought, and to meet and get to know her. Ayn Rand took a special interest in students of her philosophy who were planning careers in academic philosophy, and I had frequent access to her to discuss philosophical issues. As a young instructor, I attended the three workshops she gave in New York City in 1969 and 1970 on her monograph, *Introduction to Objectivist Epistemology*. I was the main questioner leading off the third session. I participated as well in several subsequent smaller workshops that she held in her apartment not long after the initial three. I have taught her philosophical ideas and her works in many of my courses since my earliest teaching days, and have given whole courses on her philosophy several times. I have lectured extensively on her thought at colleges and universities and to private groups in North America, in several European countries and in Japan. In 1987 I helped found The Ayn Rand Society, a professional organization affiliated with the American Philosophical Association, Eastern Division; since 1990 I have held its highest office.

In this book I speak only for myself, and express only my own understanding of Ayn Rand's thought. But I have taken pains to draw on the background I have described in order to present an accurate introduction to her philosophy—one that she would recognize and I believe approve, and which meets the needs of my audiences.

Acknowledgments

I thank Daniel Kolak, editor of the series, for his interest in the book, and for convincing me that I could finish it in time, notwithstanding a medically difficult summer. Leonard Peikoff's magisterial *Objectivism: The Philosophy of Ayn Rand* (Dutton 1991) has been of great help during the writing. Michael Berliner, Executive Director of the Ayn Rand Institute, kindly supervised the checking of biographical information for me in the Institute's Ayn Rand Archives. I received helpful comments on an earlier draft from a number of friends and colleagues, but I would like to single out Harry Binswanger, whose comments on each chapter were especially valuable. Many friends have given me both great encouragement and what is sometimes the best help one can give: to leave me in seclusion to reflect and to write.

This book is dedicated to the memory of Ayn Rand, for her inspiration and her genius.

Introduction

When she opened her eyes, she saw sunlight, green leaves and a man's face. She thought: I know what this is. This was the world as she had expected to see it at sixteen—and now she had reached it—and it seemed so simple, so unastonishing, that the thing she felt was like a blessing pronounced upon the universe by means of three words: But of course.

She was looking up at the face of a man who knelt by her side, and she knew that in all the years behind her, *this* was what she would have given her life to see: a face that bore no mark of pain or fear or guilt. The shape of his mouth was pride, and more: it was as if he took pride in being proud. The angular planes of his cheeks made her think of arrogance, of tension, of scorn—yet the face had none of these qualities, it had their final sum: a look of serene determination and of certainty, and the look of a ruthless innocence which would not seek forgiveness or grant it. It was a face that had nothing to hide or to escape, a face with no fear of being seen or of seeing, so that the first thing she grasped about him was the intense perceptiveness of his eyes—he looked as if his faculty of sight were his best-loved tool and its exercise were a limitless, joyous adventure, as if his eyes imparted a superlative value to himself and to the world—to himself for his ability to see, to the world for being a place so eagerly worth seeing. It seemed to her for a moment that she was in the presence of a being who was pure consciousness—yet she had never been so aware of a man's body. The light cloth of his shirt seemed to stress, rather than to hide, the structure of his figure, his skin was sun-tanned, his body had the hardness, the gaunt, tensile strength, the clean precision of a foundry casting, he looked as if he were poured out of metal, but some dimmed, soft-lustered metal, like an aluminum-copper alloy, the color of his skin blending with the chestnut-brown of his hair, the loose strands of the hair shading from brown to gold in the sun, and his eyes completing the colors, as the one part of the casting left undimmed and harshly lustrous: his eyes were the deep, dark green of light glinting on metal. He was looking down at her with the faint trace of a smile, it was not a look of discovery, but of familiar contemplation—as if he, too, were seeing the long-expected and the never-doubted.

This was her world, she thought, this was the way men were meant to be and to face their existence—and all the rest of it, all the years of ugliness and struggle were only someone's senseless joke. She smiled at him, as at a fellow conspirator, in relief, in deliverance, in radiant mockery of all the things she would never have to consider important again. He smiled in answer, it was the same smile as her own, as if he felt what she felt and knew what she meant.

"We never had to take any of it seriously, did we?" she whispered.

"No, we never had to."

So begins Part III of Ayn Rand's majestic *Atlas Shrugged* (1957), crown jewel of the corpus of writings whose philosophic content we are about to explore. This passage captures the essence of her view both of the world and of human possibility—and its central themes go a long way toward explaining the source of her enormous appeal as well as the hostility her works have sometimes generated. It also provides us entry into the whole of her philosophic system, and we will here take advantage of that fact.

Hallmarks of Ayn Rand's philosophic vision

Like Ayn Rand's heroine, Dagny Taggart, we too are transported from the concrete to the abstract, from the vision of this man to the human possibility he represents, a vision of man with "no mark of pain or fear or guilt." The focus is on a state of soul, the way men—and women—are "meant to be and to face their existence." The passage is only a moment in Dagny's and our introduction to John Galt, the leading character in *Atlas Shrugged*, but it is enough to show us that central to Ayn Rand's philosophic vision is a *heroic view of man*. This is a heroism of soul, i.e., of character and basic values—and we will need to explain what virtues of character and what way of facing the world make that state possible, according to Ayn Rand.

This vision of the greatness possible to man began to form early in Ayn Rand's life. In the afterword to *Atlas Shrugged*, she wrote:

> I have held the same philosophy I now hold, for as far back as I can remember. I have learned a great deal through the years and expanded my knowledge of details, of specific issues, of definitions, of applications—and I intend to keep expanding it—but I have never had to change any of my fundamentals. My philosophy, in essence, is the concept of man as a heroic being, with his own happiness as the moral purpose of his life, with productive achievement as his noblest activity, and reason as his only absolute.

Note the centrality of "the concept of man as a heroic being." All the rest is elaboration, indicating the moral values and cognitive commitment that define and make possible that heroic stature.[1] This view of human possibility, for Dagny in our passage, and for Ayn Rand, is part and parcel of a certain view of the world—a world of "sunlight [and] green leaves", a benevolent world open to man's achievement and success. This is a world in which great things are possible, and in which happiness, though requiring a demanding moral commitment, is the norm, the to-be-expected, and suffering is the accidental, "to be fought and thrown aside, not to be accepted as part of one's soul and as a permanent scar across one's view of existence."[2] We shall have to explore both the precise meaning of this claim (which is easily misunderstood) and its philosophic basis, but its centrality to Ayn Rand's thought is unmistakable. She even gave it a name: *the benevolent universe premise.*

These two propositions—the benevolent universe premise and the heroic view of man—are hallmarks of Ayn Rand's philosophic vision, and are key, I believe, to her enormous world-wide appeal. And an angry rejection of these propositions may well explain some of the startling intensity of the animus towards her one sometimes observes, especially among intellectuals of a very different sense of life, who insist that her works appeal only to adolescents (in age or spirit), and that they are superficial, or even dangerous. For if, in the words of Bertrand Russell,

The life of Man is a long march through the night, surrounded by invisible foes, tortured by weariness and pain, towards a goal that few can hope to reach, and where none may tarry long;

and other human beings

are fellow-sufferers in the same darkness, actors in the same tragedy as ourselves,[3]

and if A.E. Housman was right that we are each

a stranger and afraid / In a world [we] never made;[4]

then we had better soon get rid of fantasies of heroic selves and benevolent worlds. And so too had we better get rid of them, if the truth is, as yet others think, somewhere well in between the views of Russell (or Housman) and Ayn Rand.

But how are we to decide this issue? What *is* the truth of the matter? That, Ayn Rand holds, is a question for philosophy, even if contemporary philosophers have, on the whole, given it far too little attention. For her, the benevolent universe premise and the heroic view of man are profound truths—but they are not philosophic primaries. They rest on an entire philosophic system, and our task in this book will be to explore the key tenets of that system, and the support that Ayn Rand has offered for them. Then, in the light of that understanding, we will be in a position to return, in the final chapter, to those key propositions, for a much fuller exploration both of their content and of her reasons for holding them to be true.

Elements of the philosophic system

We can already see some of the elements of that system in the portrait of John Galt with which we began, and these elements will point to the structure of this book. Note that:

the first thing she grasped about him was the intense percep-tiveness of his eyes—he looked as if his faculty of sight were his best-loved tool and its exercise were a limitless, joyous adventure, as if his eyes imparted a superlative value to himself and to the world—to himself for his ability to see, to the world for being a place so eagerly worth seeing.

The world is there, it exists, it is *objective*. It is not created by one's mind but is there to be *seen*, to be *discovered*, by the mind. Sometimes called "metaphysical realism", this thesis, which Ayn Rand herself called "the primacy of existence", is at the center of her basic view of reality, her *metaphysics*.

Galt's perceptiveness extends of course to the rational judgments he makes on the basis of his sight, and his other senses, and it is "a limitless, joyous adventure." Knowledge, then, is possible to man—indeed Ayn Rand's profound epistemological optimism is manifest here—and is acquired through the fullest, *objective* use of reason opera-ting on the material provided by the senses. Her theoretical analysis of *reason* is at the center of Ayn Rand's view of the nature and means of knowledge, her *epistemology*.

But this full and loving commitment to reason—which she called "rationality"—is here presented as a *virtue* and as a source of *pride*. It brings with it a ruthless commitment to discovering the facts and to acting on them—an *independence* and *integrity*—and calls, especially in the realm of moral judgment, for an *honesty* and *justice*. All these traits of character in some central way serve Galt's *life*—already one can't imagine this man abandoning his own happiness to live self-sacrificially for others. And yet one can sense, at the end of the passage, in his response to her first words, his kindness to Dagny and his gentleness, part and parcel of the deeply benevolent view of the world expressed in that answer. This morality of *rational self-interest*, deriving *objective* values and virtues from the objective requirements of human survival, is at the center of Ayn Rand's *ethics*.

These three branches of philosophy—metaphysics, epistemology, ethics—are the central ones for Ayn Rand; positions on issues in all other areas depend on positions on fundamental issues in one or more of these branches. Ethics itself depends on metaphysics and epistemology, as we will see in a later chapter.[5]

Note that fundamental to her views in each of these three main branches is a thesis about *objectivity*: in metaphysics, that the world exists independently of the mind; in epistemology, that knowledge is to be achieved by strict adherence to rules of rational processing determined by reality and by the identity of man's consciousness; in ethics, that values are to be defined by reference to facts of reality, especially by reference to the facts of human nature. One of the most fundamental and distinctive elements of Ayn Rand's thought will be her analysis of *objectivity* as a relationship between human consciousness and existence that respects both the identity of consciousness and the absolutism of reality. To get fully clear on this later we will need the better part of a chapter, but we can already begin to understand why she came to call her philosophy *Objectivism*.

The structure of this book

"Formally, I call it Objectivism," Ayn Rand liked to say, "but informally I call it a philosophy for living on earth."[6] In fact, her working title for a planned book on her system was: *Objectivism: A Philosophy for Living on Earth.*[7] This statement reflected several sentiments—that philosophy serves a central and practical human need, that this role is philosophy's very reason for being, and that for the most part philosophers have failed to meet that need. It will help, then, in understanding her own system if we understand the fundamental questions that she saw philosophy as needing to answer. So, after an extended look at Ayn Rand's life and intellectual development, we will give over a chapter to her view of philosophy—what the discipline is and why we all need it. We will then turn to the foundation of her thought, outlining across two chapters her key metaphysical theses— including the primacy of existence, mentioned above—and the validation she offered for them.

The next two chapters we will devote to the Objectivist epistemology, giving attention both to her theory of perception and, at greater length, to her original theory of concepts and its implications for such issues as definition, essence, and objectivity. This account of reason as man's means of knowledge will play a key role in the account, in the following chapter, of Ayn Rand's view of man—those fundamentals of human nature which provide the bridge from metaphysics and epistemology to ethics. Three will be central: that man is a living being; that reason is his basic means of survival, and that the exercise of reason is volitional. This includes her original theory of free will and her view of the respective roles of reason, emotion, and desire in human motivation.

From here we will move into the Objectivist ethics, exploring across two chapters how Ayn Rand derives an objective theory of value from these basic facts of human nature. We will see, in short, the foundation and structure of her ethical theory; its cardinal values and moral virtues; its principles governing the proper relations among human beings; and the nature and basis of its radically original form of ethical egoism. Since she held that romantic love, properly understood, is a great source of human happiness, we will give attention as well to her view of the nature and value of love and the meaning of sex.

Ayn Rand's moral theory and its underlying conception of man provide the basis for her *politics*. In the space available in this book we will only be able to touch on her views, but we will indicate (toward the end of chapter 10) her theory of the nature and source of individual rights and her advocacy of laissez-faire capitalism as the only *moral* social system.

While she recognized specialized areas of philosophy, such as philosophy of science, law, history, education, etc. (largely as applications of epistemology, and sometimes other branches as well, to particular human disciplines), Ayn Rand singled out the philosophy of art, *esthetics*, as a major branch, alongside of metaphysics, epistemology, ethics, and politics. This was because she held that, as against these specialized disciplines, art serves a *general* need of human existence, closely allied with, but yet importantly distinct from, the need served by philosophy. Also for reasons of space we can only touch on her esthetics, but we will indicate briefly (at the end of chapter 10) her view of the nature of art, its role in human life, and the consequent availability of objective standards for defining art itself and for evaluating specific works of art.

Having surveyed the essentials of her philosophic system, we will, as already mentioned, return in our final chapter to the benevolent universe premise and the heroic view of man for a fuller understanding of their meaning, their grounds, and their relationship to the rest of Ayn Rand's philosophy.

A suggestion

Ayn Rand was a strikingly original thinker. One consequence of that fact is the need to understand her in her own terms. Readers must take her words in context, and understand her definitions and her reasons for them. One mustn't assume that she means by some words just what those words would mean if one said them oneself, or if some other philosopher did.

The most familiar example is her conception of *selfishness*. The ordinary connotation, of someone blindly insensitive to the existence or rights of others, who would "trample over others" if he thought he could "get away with it," bespeaks, in her view, an incredibly distorted sense of what is actually in a human being's interest. We have already glimpsed how far this is from her own conception of human self-interest. The traditional usage reflects both a moral antagonism towards the pursuit of self-interest and a corrupt view of what *is* in a person's interest—and so leaves us, Ayn Rand observed, without a neutral term for a passionate, rational commitment to one's own self-interest. But it is a fact that some of a person's actions will be in his interest and others not, and it is crucial to conceptualize that fact. And so she retains the term, and rejects the common connotation, titling her collection of essays on ethics *The Virtue of Selfishness: A New Concept of Egoism*.

As we proceed, we will see many other examples of how her insistence on grounding a concept in the facts of reality that give rise to our need for it, results in a radically original understanding of that concept, from *objectivity* in epistemology to *romanticism* in esthetics.

In general, readers familiar with the history of philosophy should be prepared to find Ayn Rand challenging fundamental premises that many philosophers have taken for granted (e.g., the assumption, common since Kant, that a successful epistemology could not be provided that would support metaphysical realism; or the equation of a person's interests with the satisfaction of his desires). We may each of us wish to heed the injunction of Hugh Akston, John Galt's philosophy professor in *Atlas Shrugged*, to "check your premises"—all the way down and all the way across the philosophical spectrum.

Endnotes

Full particulars about all works cited with abbreviated titles in the endnotes throughout this book are given in the Bibliography at the end of this book. A list of abbreviations used in the endnotes may be found on the last page of the Bibliography.

1. See also her lecture, "The Goal of My Writing", given in 1963 on the occasion of her receipt of an honorary doctor of letters degree from Lewis and Clark College. Speaking of her fiction she begins: "The motive and purpose of my writing *is the projection of an ideal man.*" (*Romantic Manifesto* 161, pb 162.). And near the end she states, "The motive and purpose of my writing can best be summed up by saying that if a dedication page were to precede the whole of my work, it would read: To the glory of Man." (*RM,* 174, pb 172.) See too the discussion of "man-worship" in the Introduction to the 25th anniversary edition of *The Fountainhead* (and in ch. 11 below). Elsewhere she says, focusing in effect on the last phrase in the afterword's summary statement of her philosophy ("reason as his only absolute"), that "This—the supremacy of reason—was, is and will be the primary concern of my work, and the essence of Objectivism." ("Brief Summary", *The Objectivist,* Sept. 1971, 1.)
2. *Atlas Shrugged,* 959-60, pb 883.
3. "A Free Man's Worship", *The Collected Papers of Bertrand Russell*, vol. 12 (London: Routledge, 1985).
4. *Last Poems* XII, *The Collected Poems of A. E. Housman* (New York: Holt, Rinehart & Winston, 1965.
5. Her insistence on the primacy of metaphysics and especially epistemology put her at odds with much other 20th century philosophy, both analytic and recent continental, in which issues in the philosophy of language are held to be primary. Why she held epistemology to be prior to the philosophy of language is suggested in ch. 7, n. 11.
6. *Philosophy: Who Needs It*, 12, pb 31.
7. *Journals*, 697.

1

Life and Intellectual Development (1905-43)

Early years (1905-21)

Ayn Rand was born Alisa Rosenbaum in St. Petersburg, Russia, on February 2, 1905.[1] The oldest of three daughters of middle class, cultured, largely non-observant Jewish parents, she exhibited a precocious and independent intelligence from a very young age. The earliest photographs of her show the same large bright piercing eyes that those who met her in adulthood often commented on.[2]

Her earliest moral inspiration came from the heroes of the French children's magazines she read—men of intelligence, independence and courage. These stories sparked in her a desire to invent tales of her own, of equal excitement and heroic adventure. Later she was inspired by the grandeur and the literary brilliance (if not always the image of the hero) in the novels of Victor Hugo. Her own growing sense of the joy that was life's essence she found first in the light-hearted concert band music of the time, then in the immense gaiety of the operettas of Kálmán, Lehár and Millöcker, then in the vision of "abroad" in American movies.

Always intensely curious, she worked to understand the world around her, and to articulate the ideas behind her early responses to the heroic and the benevolent. At age 12 she sought to understand what

12

appeared to be distinctive in her own method of thinking. She noticed that she was beginning to "think in principles"— formulating general statements and supporting them with chains of "why"s, which appeared to her to be the "adult" way of thinking. At age 13 she decided that she was an atheist. She thought the concept of a God, against whose arbitrary "perfection" people inevitably fell short, was completely unfounded and degrading to man, whose heroic potential she had, from her earlier readings, endorsed and conceptualized. Her favorite subjects in high school were mathematics and logic.

She thought that she wanted her life to be happy, exciting, and lived in accordance with her own judgments—that no one had the right to tell her (or anyone) that she had a duty to live for others. This, she thought as a teenager, was the real evil of the communism taking over around her in Russia: that it told the individual to live for the state, and it defined the state in terms of the unheroic masses, to which the heroic individuals—those of character, intellect and ability—were to be sacrificed.[3]

At University (1921-24)

Ayn Rand had decided at age 9 that she wanted to be a writer, to invent stories of her own heroes in adventures of her own choosing. Entering the University of Petrograd (soon to be renamed "Leningrad") at age 16, she majored in history, as she later said, "in order to get a factual knowledge of man's past, for my future writing", and minored in philosophy, "in order to achieve an objective definition of my values."[4] Plato, Christianity, Hegel, and Marx, she quickly came to despise; Aristotle and Nietzsche were exciting discoveries.

In Aristotle she found a definition of the method of thought she had gradually been developing on her own—the principle of non-contradiction (and the self-refuting character of its denial), the basing of knowledge in sense-perception, the view of concepts as abstractions from perceptual data, and probably the axiomatic structure of developed bodies of knowledge.[5] Although she admired the general this-worldly character of Aristotle's metaphysics, she found much to disagree with, and she probably did not find her sense of the heroic in his ethics.

Her awareness of her budding philosophical uniqueness is reflected in a bold, prophetic remark she made to her professor of ancient philosophy. On the course's oral final exam she was disappointed to be asked only about Plato. Her answers earned her the highest grade possible, but her professor, discerning her lack of sympathy with Plato, asked her why she disagreed with him. "My philosophical views," she said, "are not part of the history of philosophy yet. But they will be."

She was introduced to Nietzsche by a cousin, who informed her that "he beat you to all of your ideas," and reading *Thus Spoke Zarathustra*, she thought she had, in some respects, found a kindred spirit.[6] Nietzsche revered the heroic in man, he urged men to great purposes for their own happiness, he defended egoism, he condemned altruism, and he opposed the glorification of mediocrity. On the other hand, there was too much emphasis on feeling over reason, she thought, Nietzsche was too preoccupied with condemning the negative, and his praise of power made her uncomfortable, although it could, she supposed, be taken metaphorically, as a reference to spiritual power.

As she read on in Nietzsche, especially the rejection in *The Birth of Tragedy* of the Apollonian rational ideal, her sense of difference intensified. But Nietzsche was still for her a poet and philosopher of individualism, and it is possible to trace in her earlier works up through *Anthem* (1938) occasional literary echoes of his writings, and some Nietzschean elements, which by the completion of *The Fountainhead* (1943), she had come to thoroughly reject. Indeed, the contrast between her hero, Howard Roark, and the character, Gail Wynand, became her portrait of the difference between her own heroic vision and Nietzsche's.[7]

To America, with love (1924-35)

Following graduation in 1924, Ayn Rand enrolled in the All-Union State Institute of Cinematography to improve her ability to write for the screen. Two booklets she wrote in Russian in 1925, one on the actress Pola Negri and one on the movie industry in Hollywood, were recently discovered and published.[8]

Hating life in the Soviet Union, she jumped at the opportunity, which opened suddenly in 1926, to emigrate to America. From the vision of America's freedom, optimism, and gaiety provided by her readings and her film-going, she thought that here she would find a philosophic home. Soon after arriving in the United States, she took the name "Ayn Rand".[9]

After a six months' stay with relatives in Chicago, she moved on to Hollywood and, through a chance meeting with Cecil B. DeMille, secured a job at DeMille Studios, first as an extra, then as a junior writer. It was on the set of one film that she met Frank O'Connor, actor and later artist, who was to be her husband for 50 years until his death in 1979.

She worked to master the English language, read extensively, wrote when she could, mainly short stories, and projected possible longer works.[10]

In 1929 or 1930 she began work towards her first novel, *We the Living*, published six years later. Set in Soviet Russia, it showed how a statist system of any sort destroys its best individuals, those with a proud, independent will to think and *live*. Its deeper theme is the supreme value—the sacredness—of such an individual spirit and the unutterable evil of any system that would sacrifice it.[11] The book was not immediately successful; by the time word of mouth created climbing sales, the publisher had destroyed the type, and it could not be reprinted. *We the Living* was re-issued in 1959, after the success of *Atlas Shrugged*, with corrections to grammar and word-choice, and some cuts, including the omission of some vaguely Nietzschean-sounding lines that were philosophically confusing.

Forging a philosophic vision (1935-43)

As *We the Living* went to press, Ayn Rand began planning her next novel, which was to become *The Fountainhead*. It was conceived as a portrait of her distinctive conception of individualism. Her first notes on the novel are headed with an epigraph from Nietzsche, ending with the words: *"The noble soul has reverence for itself."* The notes begin: "The first purpose of this book is *a defense of egoism in its real meaning.*" The story traces the life of an architect of genius, Howard Roark, a man of "self-sufficient ego", who must do battle against various elements in society, including the woman he loves, to stay true to his values and to that self. He is the true egoist, who sees through his own eyes, and seeks his survival, his sense of his self-worth, and his happiness through his own rational, creative efforts—the man who lives *from* himself and *for* himself.

He, as a "creator", is contrasted with various "second-handers", who seek in one way or another to live through others. There is Peter Keating, who seeks greatness in other people's eyes, the self*less* man who gets his ideas and his sense of self-worth from others, and who will manipulate, deceive and do worse to achieve these ends. There is

Gail Wynand, the man "not born to be a second-hander", who goes after power, and realizes eventually that he has lost his soul in the process. And there is Ellsworth Toohey, the "humanitarian" preacher of altruism, who lives off the suffering of others and seeks to destroy greatness wherever he sees it.[12]

Dominique Francon, the lead female character, who shares Roark's spiritual self-sufficiency and his values, is presented as someone who believes that greatness cannot succeed in a world of second-hand souls, and tries to stop Roark's career to prevent him from debasing and destroying himself. Roark succeeds in spite of her efforts and the efforts of others who fight against him for other reasons, and Dominique gradually realizes her philosophical error. Her characterization focuses attention on the "benevolent universe premise" we discussed earlier, which was to become a prominent element in Ayn Rand's work.

During the gestation of *The Fountainhead*, she worked on several shorter projects. These included a successful Broadway play, *Night of January 16th*, and a novelette, *Anthem*. The play is a murder mystery set in a courtroom, in which a jury chosen from the audience votes on the guilt or innocence of the suspect. The evidence was so balanced that a juror's verdict depends on how he estimates the unusual moral character and inner spirit of the suspect.

Anthem, written in a beautiful, almost poetic style, is set in a wholly collectivized, and thus technologically primitive, future, in which even the word "I" has vanished. It tells the story of a young man "born with a curse" that makes him different from his passive "brothers" (and from what the state demands)—an active mind that questions and seeks understanding, has private wishes and has no desire to meld its identity with the larger "We". Committing "the sin of preference," he longs to be assigned to "the Home of the Scholars", to pursue "the Science of Things"; instead, he is assigned by his leaders to street sweeping. Illegally, he pursues the study on his own, in secret. Inventing, after much work, a primitive electric light, he presents it eagerly to his candle-lit world, only to see it rejected as the product of evil: he has worked on it completely on his own. All along, as he experiences the joy of his mode of living, he comes increasingly to question, then to reject, the collectivist moral code of his society. He escapes into one of the forbidden "Uncharted Forests", and comes upon remnants of the earlier "Unmentionable Times". By the book's close he has reached a full discovery and articulation of the value and indeed sacredness of the self—the 'I' which thinks and wills, and creates, and whose own assertion and joy is the goal and meaning of its existence.[13]

The Fountainhead was published in 1943. In its climax Howard Roark discovers that a housing project he had designed only on condition that it be built just as he designed it has been disfigured throughout. Having no recourse to the courts, he blows it up while it is still uninhabited and waits to face trial. The issue, he asserts, in a moving trial speech, is "a man's right to exist for his own sake." The speech, and indeed the novel in its final form, reflects a degree of maturing in Ayn Rand's philosophical thinking. We can already recognize in the speech, for instance, many of the elements and some of the structure of her final ethical theory. The heroic ideal she had forged is now seen not just as giving life meaning but as actually making life possible. The independent use of reason and the integrity of being true in action to one's rational convictions are necessities of human survival. This fact, that a human being's survival has specific requirements, now provides the basis for the definition of the human good.[14]

The novel's first aim remains ethical-psychological—the portrayal of the soul of an individualist (and the various forms of its opposite).[15] But this more metaphysical claim, that such a soul is required for human survival, begins to take center stage in her thinking and writing, and leads her, in her subsequent writings, to articulate fully the metaphysical, epistemological, and ethical-theory base of her ethical-psychological ideal.

Endnotes

1. "Alisa" is a transliteration of the Russian. The name is sometimes rendered in English as "Alissa".

2. In this paragraph and in what follows in this and the next chapter, for information about and comments by Ayn Rand, I draw on her 1960-61 biographical interviews and other material housed in the Ayn Rand Archives at the Ayn Rand Institute, Marina del Rey, CA. I have not seen or heard most of these materials personally, but have been provided the information by archivists at the Institute. See also ch. 2, n. 8.

3. This was always to be her primary objection against statism—not that it forbade subjective preference, but that it throttled and eventually destroyed the rational and heroic in man. One reason for her adult rejection of "libertarianism" was its assertion of the

value of subjective preference as such.

4. The quotations are from the afterword to *Atlas Shrugged*. Her course-work also included study of literature, biology, psychology, educational theory, social theory, political economy, and Soviet political structure. Although many of her courses were taught from a Marxist (and, more broadly, dialectical) orientation, there is no evidence that this shaped any aspect of her mature (or, for that matter, earlier) philosophical thought.

5. "The only philosophical debt I can acknowledge," she wrote almost 40 years later in the afterword to *Atlas Shrugged*, "is to Aristotle. I most emphatically disagree with a great many parts of his philosophy—but his definition of the laws of logic and of the means of human knowledge is so great an achievement that his errors are irrelevant by comparison." The three parts of *Atlas Shrugged* are titled after the three Aristotelian laws of logic, and he is referred to in Galt's speech (1016, pb 934; *FTNI*, 152-53, pb 125). She paid additional tribute to these and other aspects of Aristotle's thought in other writings. See *FTNI*, 20, pb 22; her review of John Herman Randall, Jr.'s *Aristotle* in *VOR*, ch. 2; and *The Objectivist*, August 1971, 11-12. For some perceived points of difference, see *ITOE*, 52-54; *VOS*, 3, pb 14; and the Randall review.

6. Her cousin's remark is of some interest, suggesting (as one might well expect) that Nietzsche's influence on Ayn Rand was not a matter of her absorbing whole a body of ideas new to her. Rather, Nietzsche articulated and expanded upon ideas she had already formulated and had been presenting to others—and indeed she was aware of important differences from the beginning. Nonetheless, the influence was real. (There is no evidence that her interpretation of Nietzsche was shaped by her university professors.)

7. *Zarathustra* was the first book in English Ayn Rand bought when she came to America, and she underlined her favorite passages. The clearest literary echoes are perhaps to be found in the original edition of *Anthem*. For instance, the hero, Prometheus, declares at one point that "I have broken the tables of my brothers, and my own tables do I now write for my own spirit." (1938 edn., 134). Zarathustra speaks of replacing old tables (i.e., tablets, such as the Ten Commandments were written on) with new ones in Part III, 56 "Old and New Tables". Her notes for *We the Living*, and early notes for The *Fountainhead*, suggest that for some time she may have believed with Nietzsche that heroic individuals are *born such* —or rather, since she always insisted on the existence of free will,

18

are born with a *capacity* for greatness that others are not born with, but a capacity which free choice would have to realize or embrace. (*Journals*, 51, 93; see the editor's comments on this and other Nietzschean elements, 20-22, 93, 95.) This limited innatism disappears in her 1943-45 journal entries (252-54, 289-92), where she first articulates her mature view of free will. The quotations from Nietzsche that she was planning as epigraphs for the novel as a whole and probably each of its parts (*Journals*, 77, 219) were removed in the final drafts. She explained that this was "because of my profound disagreement with [his] philosophy," including his innatist determinism (Introd. to the 25th anniv. edn. of *The Fountainhead*, xii-xiii, pb x). The more fully she defined her own ethics, epistemology and metaphysics, including her conception of man, her view of free will, and her benevolent universe premise, the more strikingly fundamental she came to see the differences between herself and Nietzsche to be. (See, e.g., *FTNI*, 39, pb 36.)

8.   *Russian Writings on Hollywood* (1999).

9.   The name "Rand" is used by Ayn Rand's sister, Nora, in a letter she sent to Ayn before Ayn's first letter reached home. Nora's letters make clear that at the time Ayn Rand left Russia she (i) had firmly chosen "Rand" and (ii) was leaning towards "Ayn" but had not yet settled on it. Her primary reason for adopting a new name (although she kept her initials) was concern that, were she to become famous under her family name, it would endanger her family. "Ayn" was modeled after a Finnish female name "Aino" or "Aina" which she liked; she probably first spotted "Rand" on a Remington Rand typewriter in Russia. ("Ayn", as the introduction to her March 1964 *Playboy* interview amusingly put it, rhymes with "mine".)

10. These and other of her unpublished writings are collected in *The Early Ayn Rand* (1984). See also *Journals*, ch. 1: The Hollywood Years, for additional scenarios and notes.

11. See the introduction to the 1959 edition of this novel, the note preceding the excerpt from the novel in *FTNI*, the excerpt itself, and *Journals*, ch. 2. In a letter written in 1934, praising an actor in a performance she saw, for "your bringing to life a completely heroic human being," she went on:

> The word *heroic* does not quite express what I mean. You see, I am an atheist and I have only one religion: the sublime in human nature. There is nothing to approach the sanctity of the highest type of man possible and there is nothing that

gives me the same reverent feeling, the feeling when one's spirit wants to kneel, bareheaded. Do not call it hero-worship, because it is more than that. It is a kind of strange and improbable white heat where admiration becomes religion, and religion becomes philosophy, and philosophy—the whole of one's life. (*Letters*, 15-16.)

Those who have read *We the Living*, and fell in love with its heroine, Kira Argounova, as I did at age 19, will understand something of what Ayn Rand meant at this time by "the highest type of man possible." The actress Alida Valli, gave a wonderful portrayal of Kira in a two-part Italian film of *We the Living* in 1943; an edited version was released in 1988 and is available on video.

12. The novel establishes, and then links, two dichotomies: the creator vs. the second-hander, and the egoist vs. the altruist. In so doing, it dramatizes an unorthodox ethical thesis of Ayn Rand's (which we will explore in a later chapter): the inseparable connection between rationality, independence and integrity on the one hand, and egoism on the other. One successfully lives *from* oneself, we might put it, if and only if one successfully lives *for* oneself.

13. One of the most poignant and beautiful lines in the book is said by the young woman, of equally unconquerable spirit, who against all rules had fallen in love with him as he with her. Trying to express herself without the singular personal pronoun, she says: "We are one...alone...and only...and we love you who are one...alone ...and only." (1946 version, ellipses in original, 50th anniv. edn., 87.) By the book's close she can say it in three words. (*Anthem* was first published in England in 1938, then in America in a corrected version in 1946. The 60th anniversary edition contains a facsimile of the copy of the 1938 edition in which she marked her changes for the 1946 edition.)

14. "The choice is not self-sacrifice or domination. The choice is independence or dependence. The code of the creator or the code of the second-hander. This is the basic issue. It rests upon the alternative of life or death. The code of the creator is built on the needs of the reasoning mind which allows man to survive. . . . All that which proceeds from man's independent ego is the good." (*The Fountainhead*, 713, pb 681.)

15. *The Fountainhead*'s theme, Ayn Rand stated, is "individualism vs. collectivism, not in politics but in man's soul; the psychological motivations and the basic premises that produce the character of an individualist or a collectivist." (*FTNI*, 77, pb 68; see also *Journals*, 223, 77-87.)

2
Life and Intellectual Development (1943-82)

Crystallizing the mature philosophy (1943-57)

Four months after the publication of *The Fountainhead*, Ayn Rand began work on a nonfiction presentation of her ethical theory (and its consequent politics), provisionally titled *The Moral Basis of Individualism*. Her notes and early drafts of three chapters have recently been edited and published as part of *Journals of Ayn Rand* (1995). Its editor is absolutely right to describe them as "a fascinating record of her philosophic development . . . in the course of [which] she is discovering and clarifying many of the ideas that become essential in John Galt's speech [in *Atlas Shrugged*]."[1]

The structure of the presentation is essentially deductive—from one axiom and several fundamental facts about man's nature. The axiom is: "Man exists and must survive as man." The fundamental facts about man's nature are: that he is a living being, that his means of survival is reason, and that the exercise of reason is a matter of *free choice*. All this is said to rest on the existence of "an objective world" and the ability of reason to know it. These facts about human nature, and their metaphysical and epistemological foundation, remain fundamental to her mature theory, and we will explore them in subsequent chapters. But the notion that ethics begins with an axiom comes to be rejected, and we can see in later notes on her first draft, the germ of her mature approach to the foundations of ethics (the bracketed remark in italics is the editor's):

> Chapter I should *begin* by stating the axiom. Then define man's nature. Then ask [*AR interrupts her thought, crossing out the preceding two words*]. Or—begin by asking whether a moral code is necessary? Prove that it is—for a rational being... (272)

This is the germ, too, of Ayn Rand's method of asking, in relation to a given concept, what facts of reality give rise to the need for that concept.[2] This method came to crystallization a few years later, when she formulated the heart of her theory of concepts,[3] from which, as we shall see in our discussion of that theory, the method directly follows.[4] In ethics, she came to decide, the fundamental concept is that of a *value*. We shall see in a later chapter how she applied this method to that concept, by asking what facts of reality give rise to the need for values and for a concept of *value*, to establish the foundations of ethics.

In 1945, Ayn Rand put aside this nonfiction project to work on her next novel, which was later to be called *Atlas Shrugged*. The idea for the novel came out of a remark she had made to a friend who was insisting it was Ayn Rand's *duty* to complete the book on ethics. Ayn Rand angrily rejected the notion. "What if I went on strike?" she said. "What if all the creative minds of the world went on strike?" She added in passing that "That would make a good novel."

Atlas Shrugged was first conceived as an essentially social-political novel. *The Fountainhead*'s theme was "individualism vs. collectivism, not in politics but in a man's soul", and had shown the nature, spirit, and value of a Howard Roark. *Atlas Shrugged* was to show how fully human existence depends on the Howard Roarks, the "prime movers", by showing what would happen were they to withdraw from the world.[5] But, her newly achieved philosophical understanding of the metaphysical, epistemological and ethical-theory foundations of her social-political claim soon fed her immense literary imagination, and the novel came to take on a breathtaking scope.

Her view of the nature and power of human reason became the novel's philosophic center. The novel dealt with the nature and volitional character of reason. It treated reason's role in shaping every aspect of human life and character, from productive activity to sex. It explored the reasoning mind's need of freedom and consequently laissez-faire capitalism, and the proper moral and economic relationships within this social system.

The novel argued that reason's abandonment by individuals and cultures was the source of all evil. But it argued, too, that evil was ultimately impotent, if left unsupported by the good, and that the good, properly defined, *could* succeed in the world, if armed with the proper philosophy—that, in that sense, we do live in a "benevolent universe". Ayn Rand offered new understandings and definitions of many of these features and dimensions of human experience, all in the course of an exciting, complex, astonishingly integrated "philosophical mystery story" with many of the grandest characters she had ever created.[6]

The novel's climax is a long, philosophical radio speech, tightly integrated into the plot, delivered by John Galt, leader of the strike. He identifies the morality of altruism and its anti-reason foundations as the source of the world's devastation, and he demands that the coercive social system built on it must be abandoned if the strikers are to return. He presents a new morality of rational self-interest based on a proper understanding of the nature of reason and its role in human life, and explains in detail the nature of the free, individual rights-respecting social-political system that it requires. The speech took Ayn Rand two years to write. It captures to an astonishing extent the full range of philosophical ideas that are dramatized in the events of the novel.

The fifteen years between the drafting of Roark's speech for *The Fountainhead* and the completion of Galt's speech in *Atlas Shrugged* had seen the crystallization and formulation of Ayn Rand's mature philosophy, Objectivism. During this period she had developed an enormously wide-ranging, integrated philosophical system. It included newly worked-out views on the relation of mind and the world, the nature of objectivity, the nature and source of concepts, the nature and case for free will, the root of objective values, the base of individual rights, the role of art in human existence, the meaning of sex—in short, the topics of the book before you.

After *Atlas Shrugged* (1957-82)

The Fountainhead had been a best-seller, and many readers spoke of it as having changed their lives. *Atlas Shrugged* launched a philosophic movement. The novel was extolled by its readers and denigrated by the critics (with rare exceptions). It was discussed everywhere, especially on college campuses. Campus clubs formed, and commentators noticed. A young psychologist, Nathaniel Branden, whose fan letter to Ayn Rand in late 1949 had resulted in a meeting and then a long period of study and friendship with her, developed, with her assistance, several courses of lectures on various aspects of her thought and its application. These, and courses by other associates in a small circle Branden formed around her, were given live in New York City and on audio tape in well over 100 cities. She received widespread media coverage, and at first gave frequent interviews.[7] In 1968, she terminated all relations with Branden (and his former wife Barbara).[8]

Following the publication of *Atlas Shrugged*, Ayn Rand turned to nonfiction, to present her philosophy and to discuss its application to current cultural and political events. First to appear was *For the New Intellectual: The Philosophy of Ayn Rand* (1961). This book collected the philosophic speeches from her four novels. Each excerpt was briefly introduced. The excerpts were preceded by a long title essay on the impact philosophers and other intellectuals have had in the course of western civilization and on the need for "new intellectuals" who will unite thought and action in a new defense of reason, individualism and capitalism.

She began lecturing at universities around the country and drew large audiences wherever she went. She edited and published (with Branden until 1968, then by herself) *The Objectivist Newsletter* (1962-65), *The Objectivist* (1966-71), and *The Ayn Rand Letter* (1971-76), for which, overall, she wrote the majority of the articles. These lectures and articles became the basis for a series of collections: *The Virtue of Selfishness: A New Concept of Egoism* (1963), *Capitalism: The Unknown Ideal* (1966), *The Romantic Manifesto: A Philosophy of Literature* (1969), *The New Left: The Anti-Industrial Revolution* (1971) and, posthumously, *Philosophy: Who Needs It* (1982) and *The Voice of Reason: Essays in Objectivist Thought* (1989).

Ayn Rand had planned to write a full-length treatise on her philosophical system, dealing predominantly with epistemology, and made some notes towards the book in 1958 and 1959.[9] She had put it aside to reach a wider audience through her periodicals and essay collections, and to deal with the application of her philosophy to cultural and political issues as well as with theoretical philosophy. However, in 1966-67 she presented her theory of concepts, the heart of her epistemological theory, in a seven-part series in *The Objectivist*, under the title *Introduction to Objectivist Epistemology*. This series was subsequently published under the same title as a monograph, first

24

by the periodical (1967) and later by New American Library (1979). The 1979 volume included a long essay, based on her theory of concepts, attacking all aspects of "the analytic-synthetic dichotomy", a philosophical doctrine about meaning and truth that has shaped much contemporary philosophy. The essay had been written in 1967, in consultation with her, by Leonard Peikoff, philosophy professor and close associate of hers for many years. Ayn Rand held several workshops on her monograph for philosophers and advanced graduate students between 1969 and 1971.[10] Extensive excerpts from the workshop were published in an expanded second edition of the book in 1990.

During the last six years of her life, after the close of *The Ayn Rand Letter*, she lectured and wrote occasionally, and assisted in several (unsuccessful) ventures aimed at producing a movie or television mini-series *of Atlas Shrugged*. She did several television and press interviews. She advised Leonard Peikoff on the development of a series of lectures on her philosophical system, which he first gave in 1976; she joined him in answering questions at some of the lectures. She discussed philosophy (and much else) actively with associates and friends. For her own pleasure and her philosophical interest, she received tutoring in algebra, picking up where she had left off in high school. She reflected further on the relationship between mathematics and concept-formation, although regrettably she did not write down her thoughts. She planned her next collection of essays, *Philosophy: Who Needs It.* Her mind was active and sharp to the end. She died of heart failure on March 6, 1982.

She had designated Leonard Peikoff as her heir. He has overseen the posthumous publication, first of the two collections of essays and unpublished fiction already mentioned, then of editions of her letters, journals, marginalia, various shorter writings, and workshop and lecture transcriptions.[11] The original manuscripts of her novels have been deposited in the Library of Congress. The Ayn Rand Institute, organized under Peikoff's supervision in 1984, has established the Ayn Rand Archives.

In 1987, The Ayn Rand Society, a professional society dedicated to "fostering the scholarly study by philosophers of the philosophical thought and writings of Ayn Rand," was formed and received affiliation with the American Philosophical Association, Eastern Division.

Those who participated in various workshops or other philosophical discussion with Ayn Rand were aware of how well-developed her philosophical thought was in many areas on which she never wrote. They sometimes took notes on these meetings and often related to each other what she had said on some philosophical topic. The more formal sessions were often taped. Leonard Peikoff sometimes lectured on such issues in public, after consultation with her, and he and others have taught that material to yet others. Although scholars and students of Ayn Rand must treat all such reports with care, this "oral tradition" also provides source material on Ayn Rand's philosophic thought. Of greatest importance in this regard is Peikoff's *Objectivism: The Philosophy of Ayn Rand* (1991). As Peikoff points out in his preface, in writing this book he relied for Ayn Rand's "most important ideas [that] are expressed only briefly or not at all in her books," on "discussions that I have had with Miss Rand across a period of decades. This is especially true of the material on metaphysics and epistemology, which were the primary subjects of our discussions, but it applies throughout." (xiv.) Furthermore, the book is an adaptation of Peikoff's 1976 lectures, already mentioned, which Ayn Rand endorsed as an accurate presentation of her philosophy. In these respects, Peikoff's book is the most important part of this "oral tradition". As such, it is not only a uniquely informed secondary work on Ayn Rand's philosophical thought, but is also a quasi-*primary* source for her thought.[12]

In what follows, we will focus on the *mature* philosophy as presented in *Atlas Shrugged* and her subsequent non-fiction writings, with occasional use of the oral tradition just referred to, of which my own recollections form a small part. We start with her view of the nature and importance of philosophy itself.

Endnotes

1. *Journals*, 243. The bulk of the surviving materials was published as *Journals,* ch. 8.
2. Above, p. 10.
3. In reflection on a conversation she'd had with a Thomist, with whose realist position on the classical problem of universals she had disagreed, while at the same time maintaining that concepts were objective. See *ITOE*, 307.
4. Below, p. 67.
5. *Journals*, 390-95.
6. She later described the novel's theme as "the role of the mind in

man's existence—and, as corollary, the demonstration of a new moral philosophy: the morality of rational self-interest." (*FTNI*, 103, pb 88.)

7. Far and away the best interview was the one with Alvin Toffler, which appeared in *Playboy*, in March 1964.

8. Her explanation was provided in *The Objectivist*, May 1968. Barbara Branden has written a biography/memoir of Ayn Rand, based in part on taped interviews with her in 1960 and 1961. The book has numerous factual errors and engages throughout in gratuitous psychologizing which seems to reflect its author's continued embitterment. Because of this, although I have consulted the book where it draws directly on the taped interviews, I have checked every report I have used (and other details of Ayn Rand's life) with archivists at the Ayn Rand Institute, which has access to all the tapes. Readers who wish additional material on Ayn Rand's life will find a sensitive, moving portrayal in the Academy Award-nominated full-length documentary film, *Ayn Rand: A Sense of Life*, directed by Michael Paxton (1997), and in the accompanying book under the same name (Gibbs-Smith, 1998). See also "My Thirty Years With Ayn Rand: An Intellectual Memoir" (1987) by Leonard Peikoff, *VOR*, Epilogue.

9. *Journals*, 697-704; see also *FTNI* vii; *ITOE* 1.

10. See above, Preface, p. 2.

11. *Letters* (1995); *Journals* (1997); *Marginalia* (1995); *Column* (1991, 1999); the expanded second edition of *ITOE* already mentioned; *The Art of Fiction* (2000), and *Non-Fiction Writing* (forthcoming). Extensive excerpts from her writings are available in *Lexicon* (1986), and *Reader* (1999).

12. There is, unfortunately, not much of serious interpretative value among the secondary material that has been published on Ayn Rand in books or academic journals to date. I will survey some of that material in an essay to be published elsewhere, and restrict myself in this book to the use of primary sources, including the "oral tradition" just discussed.

3

"A Philosophy for Living On Earth"

The three questions

In 1974 Ayn Rand was invited to lecture to the senior class at the United States Military Academy at West Point, who were all taking a required philosophy course, on the value of the study of philosophy. She chose the title, "Philosophy: Who Needs It." Speaking to an audience that included most of the cadets and faculty at the Academy, she began:

> Since I am a fiction writer, let us start with a short short story. Suppose that you are an astronaut whose spaceship gets out of control and crashes on an unknown planet. When you regain consciousness and find that you are not hurt badly, the first three questions in your mind would be: Where am I? How can I discover it? What should I do?[1]

In her story the astronaut experiences some fear, decides not to think about his plight, doubts his instruments, then finds himself with little desire to take any action; seeing some creatures of vaguely human form approaching, he decides that they will tell him what to do. The astronaut "is never heard from again." Perhaps, she said to the cadets, you would not act like that, and no astronaut would. "But this is the way most men live their lives, here, on earth."

Most men spend their days struggling to evade three questions, the answers to which underlie man's every thought, feeling and action, whether he is consciously aware of it or not: Where am I? How do I know it? What should I do?

These, she explained, are the root questions of philosophy, and it is our need of systematic, rational answers to these questions that has given rise to the discipline. What issues these questions cover, why we need answers to them, and what method will secure those answers, were addressed in the rest of her lecture.

The three main branches of philosophy

"Philosophy," she stated, "studies the *fundamental* nature of existence, of man, and of man's relation to existence." The three questions give rise to the three main branches of philosophy: Where am I?—metaphysics. How do I know it?—epistemology. What should I do?—ethics. Ethics itself rests on metaphysics and epistemology, and on a general view of man's nature which incorporates the results of these two branches. [2]

Metaphysics asks:

Are you in a universe which is ruled by natural laws and, therefore is stable, firm, absolute—and knowable? Or are you in an incomprehensible chaos, a realm of inexplicable miracles, an unpredictable, unknowable flux, which your mind is impotent to grasp? Are the things you see around you real—or are they only an illusion? Do they exist independent of any observer—or are they created by the observer? Are they the object or the subject of man's consciousness? Are they *what they are*—or can they be changed by a mere act of your consciousness, such as a wish?

Metaphysics is concerned, then, with the basic relationship between mind and the world, with the nature and extent of what is real, and with the extent to which things have identity and obey causal laws.

Epistemology, she says, builds on the fact that man is neither omniscient nor infallible. That being so, "you have to discover what you can claim as knowledge and how to *prove* the validity of your conclusions." So, epistemology asks:

> Does man acquire knowledge by a process of reason—or by sudden revelation from a supernatural power? Is reason a faculty that identifies and integrates the material provided by man's senses—or is it fed by innate ideas, implanted in man's mind before he was born? Is reason competent to perceive reality—or does man possess some other cognitive faculty which is superior to reason? Can man achieve certainty—or is he doomed to perpetual doubt?

Epistemology is concerned, then, with the nature and source of knowledge, with the nature and proper operation of reason, with reason's relation to the senses and perception, with reason's efficacy as a source of knowledge, with whether other sources of knowledge are possible, and with the nature and means of certainty.

The nature of our actions and the extent of our ambition, self-confidence, and success will be different, she suggests, according to which set of answers to the questions in the above quotations we accept. For, our answers constitute our view of what sort of world we are confronted with and with what tools we confront it.

It is from our answers to these metaphysical and epistemological questions that we form our basic view of what is possible to us in life, and the emotional counterpart of this view, our *sense of life*.[3] Our metaphysical and epistemological convictions and our view of what is possible to us, then shape our answer to the question "What should I do?" As such a being in such a world, with such possibilities as that implies, how should I live? The answer comes from ethics, which asks specifically:

> What is the good or evil for man—and why? Should man's primary concern be a quest for joy—or an escape from suffering? Should man hold self-fulfillment—or self-destruction—as the goal of his life? Should man pursue his values—or should he place the interest of others above his own? Should man seek happiness—or self-sacrifice?

Ethics is concerned, then, with the nature and the objective foundation of the good, with the fundamental values man should pursue, with the moral principles and states of character that are needed to achieve those values, and with who is the proper beneficiary of man's actions.[4]

"I do not have to point out," she said to the cadets, "the different consequences of these two sets of answers [in the quotation just above]. You can see them everywhere—within you and around you."

Our need of philosophy

In an earlier essay, Ayn Rand gave an elegant summary of this view of philosophy and its primary branches:

> In order to live, man must act; in order to act, he must make choices; in order to make choices, he must define a code of values; in order to define a code of values, he must know *what* he is and *where* he is—i.e., he must know his own nature (including his means of knowledge) and the nature of the universe in which he acts—i.e., he needs metaphysics, epistemology, ethics, which means: *philosophy*. He cannot escape from this need; his only alternative is whether the philosophy guiding him is to be chosen by his mind or by chance.[5]

An indication of that need, she explained to the cadets at West Point, is the extent of philosophy's influence even on those who may be tempted to dismiss it:

> Have you ever thought or said the following? "Don't be so sure—nobody can be certain of anything." You got that notion from David Hume (and many, many others), even though you might never have heard of him. Or: "This may be good in theory, but it doesn't work in practice." You got that from Plato. Or: "That was a rotten thing to do, but it's only human, nobody is perfect in this world." You got it from Augustine. Or: It may be true for you, but it's not true for me." You got it from William James.

And so on, for eight more such philosophical catch-phrases, including that one needn't "believe that stuff *all* of the time," because "It may have been true yesterday, but it's not true today" (which, she said, people got from Hegel).[6]

But what is the source of that need? Why must we hold our answers to the questions of philosophy in the form of *principles*? And why do we need to decide on our answers consciously and rationally and with the rigorous discipline involved in a proper study of philosophy?

The influence which philosophical catch-phrases have on us, she explained, is a sign of the fact that as human beings we can function only by "integrating [our] observations, [our] experiences, [our] knowledge into...principles." Otherwise we would, in effect, be "in the position of a newborn infant, to whom every object is a unique, unprecedented phenomenon." We cannot avoid generalizing from past experience, forming principles, in order to anticipate and deal with new situations. "Your only choice," she said:

> Is whether these principles are true or false, whether they represent your conscious rational convictions—or a grab-bag of notions snatched at random, whose sources, validity, context and consequences you do not know, notions which, more often than not, you would drop like a hot potato if you knew.

If we don't think for ourselves, we will absorb ideas passively from people and institutions around us, with little clue as to their ultimate source and validity.

Likewise we need to *integrate* our principles—to unite our conclusions about the world, about ourselves, about the values to pursue, and so on, into a logically coherent whole.

> What integrates them? Philosophy. A philosophic system is an integrated view of existence. As a human being, you have no choice about the fact that you need a philosophy. Your only choice is whether you define your philosophy by a conscious, rational, disciplined process of thought and scrupulously logical deliberation—or let your subconscious accumulate a junk heap of unwarranted conclusions, false generalizations, undefined contradictions, undigested slogans, unidentified wishes, doubts and fears, thrown together by chance, but integrated by your subconscious into a kind of mongrel philosophy and fused into a single, solid weight: *self-doubt*, like a ball and chain in the place where your mind's wings should have grown.

Letting oneself be guided by emotions, she went on to explain, is no alternative to a scrupulously rational method. Our emotions reflect our subconsciously held values and view of life—the philosophy we have already acquired, either by thought or by chance. If we refuse to give attention to philosophy we will be programmed by ideas over which we have no control—we will be blind to the world and to ourselves and will fear both.[7]

To answer these questions, then, we need a strict rational discipline. We need a scrupulous loyalty to observed facts. We need a firm commitment to the non-contradictory identification of those facts. We need to build our conclusions step by logical step. We need to identify the fundamentals on any issue. We need to work back to the primary principles in any area and to their validation. We need, in short, the skills and the discipline which *philosophy* can teach us—or should.

We need to learn from those philosophers who have some truth to teach us, and we have to learn to detect the falsehoods and fallacies in the works of the many philosophers who don't. Indeed, because of philosophy's profound power to shape lives, understanding what is wrong in influential philosophical traditions that are mistaken and why is a matter of "self-protection". But most of all, we need to learn how to discover what is true. And so, concluding her argument and making a transition to the tribute to West Point with which she ended her lecture, she said:

> Nothing is given to man automatically, neither knowledge, nor self-confidence, nor inner serenity, nor the right way to use his mind. Every value he needs or wants has to be discovered, learned and acquired—even the proper posture of his body. In this context, I want to say that I have always admired the posture of West Point graduates, a posture that projects man in proud, disciplined control of his body. Well, philosophical training gives man the proper *intellectual* posture—a proud, disciplined control of his mind.

So, philosophy is, in a very deep sense, for Ayn Rand (and for us), a life-and-death matter. And working out a rational philosophy for oneself is a crucial responsibility for each human being. Philosophy, then, for her, is not an end in itself—it is an indispensable tool of man's survival and well-being.[8]

The foundation of this view of philosophy

Ayn Rand's argument, summarized above, against substituting emotions for reason in the direction of one's life is built on the premise that "emotions are not tools of cognition."[9] As she pointed out later in the lecture, one's position on the nature and need of philosophy inevitably rests on logically prior aspects of one's philosophic system. Her own position rests on at least the following philosophical theses: that there *is* a truth of the matter in these issues; that disciplined rational thought based on a scrupulous loyalty to observed facts *is* our method of acquiring truth; that emotions indeed reflect previously acquired philosophical premises; and that we human beings have an ultimate choice over our mode of cognitive functioning.

Those who find the argument of her West Point lecture convincing are implicitly accepting these theses, as well they might. But not all of these theses are self-evident and all need fuller explanation. Ayn Rand's view of our need of philosophy is integrated with and depends upon much else in her philosophic system. It is the task of what follows in this book to expound and clarify the essential tenets of that system.

In the words of her favorite philosopher, Aristotle: "Let us begin first with what is first."

Endnotes

1. *PWNI*, 1. To capture some of this event, and to give readers a taste of Ayn Rand's own way of presenting her views on this central issue, I quote extensively from the lecture throughout this chapter. All quotations in this chapter are from that lecture unless otherwise indicated.
2. If one considers that the two fundamental relations of man to the world are knowledge and action, one can connect her definition of philosophy to these three questions and to the various branches of philosophy (including politics, esthetics, and the specialized branches mentioned above, p. 9).

3. The concept of a *sense of life* and the relation of a person's sense of life to his philosophic convictions, both conscious and subconscious, are discussed by Ayn Rand in a separate article, "Philosophy and Sense of Life," *RM*, ch. 2. See also below, p. 92.

4. For the remaining branches of philosophy, on which she commented much more briefly in this lecture, see above, p. 9.

5. "Philosophy and Sense of Life," *RM* 37-38, pb 30.

6. The issue of how philosophic ideas are transmitted through a culture to "the man on the street" is discussed by Ayn Rand in the title essay of her book, *For the New Intellectual* (1961).

7. Although literary works, and works of art in general, can provide philosophical inspiration and some direction, they are likewise *not* a substitute for philosophy. The ideas and values in them that one responds to emotionally must be articulated, examined, rationally validated and creatively applied. On the place of art, especially literature, in the development of a person's philosophical orientation, see "Art and Moral Treason", *RM*, ch. 9 (with chs. 1-3).

8. Ayn Rand's view of philosophy differs, then, though subtly, from Aristotle's—since its *ultimate* justification lies in its providing a framework for *action* (and "practical" philosophy is much more closely linked, in Ayn Rand's case, to "theoretical" philosophy, in Aristotle's sense of these terms). But her view of philosophy also differs from pragmatism's, since for Ayn Rand, with her metaphysical realism, the practical purpose on which philosophy rests provides no part of the criterion of *truth*, as it does for pragmatism.

9. A fuller account of Ayn Rand's view of the nature of emotions, their relation to cognition, and their proper role in human life, will be provided in the chapter on her conception of man's nature.

4

Metaphysics

Philosophic axioms

"In order to live," Ayn Rand has said,[1] "man must . . . know *what* he is and *where* he is—i.e., he must know his own nature (including his means of knowledge) and the nature of the universe in which he acts—i.e., he needs metaphysics, epistemology, ethics, which means: *philosophy*." These are the subjects of this and the following chapters: the nature of reality, of knowledge, of man, of value, and of the values man must choose in order to live. The nature of reality—of existence —is first.

Ayn Rand insisted that there are proper starting points in philosophy. This is because all human knowledge is hierarchical and rests on the grasp of certain basic facts about existence and consciousness. As such, these facts form the foundation of metaphysics and epistemology as well, so that the identification of the facts and concepts at the foundation of human knowledge in general give us the starting points of these two branches and, thus, of all of philosophy.[2]

Following Aristotle, Ayn Rand calls the statements of these basic facts *axioms*. "An axiom," she writes, "is a statement that identifies the base of knowledge and of any further statement pertaining to that knowledge, a statement necessarily contained in all others, whether any particular speaker chooses to identify it or not."[3]

That the acceptance of axioms is inescapable provides an objective method for establishing that a statement is axiomatic, if indeed it is. The method consists in showing that the statement's "opponents . . .

36

have to accept it and use it in the process of any attempt to deny it."[4] This method is sometimes called "re-affirmation through denial".

Proving that a statement is an *axiom* establishes its place in the hierarchy of knowledge—establishes that it is an axiom. It is not meant to prove that it is true. An axiom's truth *needs no proof.* The facts that axioms state are, as we will see momentarily, self-evident in perception; and all proof is based on a prior acceptance of the axioms.[5]

There are three basic axioms, Ayn Rand holds: existence, consciousness, and identity. We will explore each of these, their status as axioms, and their relations to each other. We will then draw out some of their implications—for causality, for the relation of mind and body, and for the rejection of the "supernatural"—and conclude with a brief overview of Ayn Rand's metaphysics.

Existence, Consciousness, Identity

The simplest and most basic fact about the world, for children or adults, is that *something exists.* Well before a baby could perceptually differentiate one thing in its field of awareness from another, it is aware, wordlessly, that there is—*something.* Something *exists.* This is the first thing grasped and it remains the most fundamental.

Suppose that a philosophy professor were to announce in class that after years of study he has discovered that *nothing exists.* What would your reaction be? You might observe that his statement is not only false, it is *self-refuting.* In order for such a statement to be made, the statement's speaker must exist, its content must exist, and some sort of world must exist to give meaning to that content. If nothing existed, you might remark, there would be no one there to notice it. What is perceptually self-evident and absolutely undeniable is that *something exists.*

We start with existence—that which is—and the first thing we recognize about it is: that it *is.* In Ayn Rand's words: "*existence exists*". This is *the axiom of existence,* and it is the first philosophic axiom.[6] Its axiomatic status is clear from our discussion of the professor: any attempt to deny that something exists accepts and uses the fact that something does exist. This is a clear case of "re-affirmation through denial".

Your act of grasping that something exists implies a second inescapable fact: that you are *conscious*—i.e., that you are *aware of what exists.* Your possession of consciousness—the faculty of perceiving what exists—is a second self-evident and undeniable fact.

Were our professor to announce that after years of study he has discovered that he is not conscious, you would rightly protest that he has to be conscious to discover that. That something exists and that one is conscious of what exists are inescapable facts at the root of all of one's knowledge. That one exists possessing consciousness is *the axiom of consciousness*, the second philosophic axiom.[7] As with the professor, any attempt to *deny* that one is conscious makes use of the fact that one *is*.[8] Again, re-affirmation through denial establishes that the statement is indeed an axiom.

Ayn Rand put it all this way in John Galt's speech in *Atlas Shrugged*:

> Existence exists—and the act of grasping that statement implies two corollary axioms: that something exists which one perceives and that one exists possessing consciousness, consciousness being the faculty of perceiving that which exists.
>
> If nothing exists, there can be no consciousness: a consciousness with nothing to be conscious of is a contradiction in terms. A consciousness conscious of nothing but itself is a contradiction in terms: before it could identify itself as consciousness, it had to be conscious of something. If that which you claim to perceive does not exist, what you possess is not consciousness.
>
> Whatever the degree of your knowledge, these two— existence and consciousness—are axioms you cannot escape, these two are the irreducible primaries implied in any action you undertake, in any part of your knowledge and in its sum, from the first ray of light you perceive at the start of your life to the widest erudition you might acquire at its end. Whether you know the shape of a pebble or the structure of a solar system, the axioms remain the same: that *it* exists and that you *know* it.[9]

The order in which these two axioms are presented is crucial to Ayn Rand's thought. Existence is first, then consciousness. Consciousness, she holds, is inherently *relational*—it is *of* something that exists independent of that act of consciousness.[10] This, she holds, is self-evident—available to anyone who simply examines introspectively the phenomenon that the concept of "consciousness" refers to. Let's explore this thesis of hers by examining the contrary claim of the philosopher Descartes.

Descartes, in his own attempt to establish the foundations of knowledge, claimed that consciousness comes first. The first undeniable fact, he famously said, is: "I think therefore I am." I can doubt everything else, even the existence of an external world, but I cannot doubt that I "think" (i.e., that I am conscious).

But, Ayn Rand asks (as also Aristotle would have): what then is your consciousness aware *of*? It cannot be aware only of itself—there is no "itself" until it is aware of something. And it cannot be aware only of objects it has created, since there is nothing to do the creating before there is awareness of an independent something.[11]

Any attempt to *deny* that consciousness is awareness of objects that have an existence independent of that awareness will directly or indirectly accept that consciousness *is* awareness of independent objects.[12]

The thesis that existence comes first—that things exist independent of consciousness and that consciousness is a faculty not for the creation of its objects but for the discovery of them—Ayn Rand called *the primacy of existence*. The primacy of existence is, as we have just seen, axiomatic—but it is not a distinct axiom. It is rather a corollary or elaboration of the two axioms already presented (and of the third to come). It is central to Ayn Rand's metaphysics and to her philosophy overall, and we will return to it after we examine the third and final philosophic axiom—*identity*.

Here is how the axiom of identity is introduced in John Galt's speech in a passage that follows immediately upon the passage just quoted, which presented the first two axioms:

> To exist is to be something, as distinguished from the nothing of non-existence, it is to be an entity of a specific nature made of specific attributes. Centuries ago, the man who was—no matter what his errors—the greatest of your philosophers, has stated the formula defining the concept of existence and the rule of all knowledge: *A is A*. A thing is itself. . . Existence is Identity, Consciousness is Identification.
>
> Whatever you choose to consider, be it an object, an attribute or an action, the law of identity remains the same. A leaf cannot be a stone at the same time, it cannot be all red and all green at the same time, it cannot freeze and burn at

39

the same time. A is A. Or, if you wish it stated in simpler language: You cannot have your cake and eat it, too.[13]

What exists primarily are *entities*, and entities have *identity*. The *identity* of an entity is the sum of its attributes or characteristics—everything that it is, including its capacities for change.[14]

In connection with this axiom, we might imagine our professor announcing to the class that he has something fascinating at home. "What is it?" you ask (drawing on your implicit acceptance that everything is *something*). "That's what's so fascinating," he replies. "It isn't *anything*. It's not big or little, not heavy or light, not solid or liquid or gaseous, not physical or even mental. It isn't *anything*—it doesn't have any attributes at all. Want to buy it?" Your response might well be that there can *be* no such thing. To *be*, you might say, is to be *something*. What difference is there, you might ask, between something not having any attributes and it not existing at all? Existence, as Ayn Rand put it, *is* Identity.[15]

In that sense, an entity *is* its attributes—there is no bare "substratum" that possesses them (which is why Ayn Rand, in the passage just quoted, described an entity as "made of specific attributes"). An entity is not, however, a "bundle" of attributes; it is a whole, a unity, of which its attributes are aspects.

In the concept's primary sense an *entity* is a solid object with a perceivable shape, which acts or resists action as a whole. The beginnings of cognition, at the perceptual level, involve the grasp that the "somethings" out there are distinguishable things, *entities*, and the concept is basic to all subsequent cognition. In relation to the three axioms, "entity" is best thought of not as a separate axiom but as a specification of, or category under, existence.[16]

Existence, Consciousness, Identity. These are the basic facts (and concepts) at the root of all knowledge, according to Ayn Rand. For there to be knowledge, there must be something to know (Existence), someone to know it (Consciousness), and something to know about it (Identity). These are the three philosophic axioms.[17]

Although these axioms are self-evident, we do not automatically take them into account, and so it may be necessary to remind oneself of them. Consider someone who says, in response to a difficult situation: "I don't want to think about it," and pushes his hand outward as if to ward off the unpleasant reality. His implicit premise is that if he doesn't think about the problem, it won't exist. But, as the axiom of existence would remind this person, that's not so. If the problem exists, it *exists*. Wishing things away won't make them go away (Existence), nor will wishing them to be different change *what* they are (Identity).

If one wants to change the world, one needs to take action *in* the world. But to change something in the world, one needs to know what sort of action is required to produce that change *given the thing's identity*. As Ayn Rand liked to quote from Francis Bacon: "Nature, to be commanded, must be obeyed." In respecting existence and identity, one must also respect causality—and that brings us to the next major topic of Ayn Rand's metaphysics.[18]

Endnotes

1. Above, p. 31.
2. Ayn Rand's thesis that human knowledge is both hierarchical and contextual will be discussed in the chapters on epistemology.
3. *AS*, 1040, pb 956; *FTNI*, 193, pb 155. For Aristotle's use of the term, see his *Metaphysics*, book IV, ch. 3.
4. *AS*, 1040, pb 956; *FTNI*, 193, pb 155. Aristotle was the first to define and use this method to establish the axiomatic status of the law of non-contradiction, in his *Metaphysics*, book IV, chs. 3-4.
5. See Peikoff, *OPAR*, 8.
6. Ayn Rand here uses "existence" as a collective noun, for all that which exists taken together. And she subsumes under this concept "everything—every entity, action, attribute, relationship (including every state of consciousness)—everything which is, was, or will be." (Peikoff, *OPAR*, 5.)
7. The question of the relation of consciousness to its physical correlates or conditions is irrelevant to this point. What is axiomatic is the *fact* of consciousness—i.e., its existence and its cognitive efficacy. Any analysis of the *conditions* of consciousness that results in a denial of the *fact* of consciousness is self-refuting.
8. Denials of the axiom of consciousness can take many forms, all self-refuting. These include claims that no one can truly know anything (which is a claim to knowledge); that no one can be certain about anything (which is a claim to certainty); that there are no absolutes (which is a claim that is itself "absolute"); and that the senses cannot be relied on to ground our knowledge (which claim relies on the use of the senses, as we will see in a later chapter).
9. *AS* 1015-16, pb 933-34; *FTNI*, 152, pb 124-25.

10. Any content of consciousness that is not a direct awareness of something that actually exists derives ultimately from some other content that *is* a direct awareness of what actually exists. (*ITOE*, 29-31.) We can, of course, be aware of our own states and processes of consciousness, but (i) those states and processes are independent of the act of self-consciousness, and (ii) they must themselves be directed upon some content outside of consciousness. In that sense even states of consciousness are "independent of consciousness"—i.e., independent of the act of consciousness by which they are grasped.

11. The independence of the object of perceptual awareness from the act of perception is thus self-evidently available to us, according to Ayn Rand. If many philosophers persist nonetheless in holding the Cartesian premise that we can be certain we are aware of *something* while doubting the existence of an external world, she held, it is because they subscribe to an erroneous theory of perception. The actually self-evident may not appear self-evident to those in the throes of wrong theory. We will return to this point in our discussion of her direct realist theory of perception in the chapter after next (p 56 with its n.2). See also the next note.

12. Many philosophers have attempted to build their systems on the denial of the existence of an independent reality. In maintaining that the independence of the real is axiomatic, Ayn Rand is in effect maintaining that every such attempt will ultimately make use of the very fact it is attempting to deny. One example familiar to philosophers is the 20th century thesis of "phenomenalism" (essentially a linguistic restatement of the subjective idealism of the 18th century philosopher, Berkeley). Phenomenalists claimed that they could analyze all statements about material objects in terms of statements about "sense-data" (i.e., internal contents of consciousness). After decades of trying without success, phenomenalists gave up (or died off), after several devastating critical essays showed that their analyses in fact could not "get rid of" space, time, or, indeed, material objects.

    Descartes did not himself deny the existence of an independent reality. Rather, like many philosophers of his time (and today), he held that we are directly aware of mental contents which "represent" an independent world and from which we may infer (or "compute") to that world. This "representative realism" could not sustain itself in the period after Descartes; it collapsed into the skepticism of David Hume and the "Copernican Revolution" of Immanuel Kant, who argued explicitly that the mind constructs the "reality" it knows. Even Kant held on to an unknowable "thing in itself" as a last vestige of a sense that an independent object must ground consciousness. But this was soon dropped by the "Idealist" tradition that followed; and we have been arguing that Idealism—the pure primacy of consciousness—is self-refuting.

13. *AS*, 1016, pb 934; *FTNI*, 152-53, pb 125. The philosopher referred to is, of course, Aristotle. (See n. 4 above.) The law of non-contradiction is for Ayn Rand a restatement, for purposes of logic, of the same fact expressed in the law of identity.

14. There are epistemological reasons why, in *stating* the identity of a thing (or attribute), we may state only the *kind* of thing (or attribute) it is or the essential properties of a thing (or attribute) of that kind, as reflected in the definition of that kind. But a thing's identity, according to Ayn Rand, is restricted neither to its being a member of a kind nor to its essential properties as a thing of that kind. Nor is there any justification for a *metaphysical* distinction between essential and non-essential properties. We will return to these issues when we discuss concepts and definition.

15. Indeed, for Ayn Rand, "existence" and "identity" conceptualize the very same fact from two perspectives. See Peikoff, *OPAR*, 7.

16. For further discussion of the concept of "entity" both in its metaphysical aspects and in its cognitive role, see *ITOE*, 5-6, 264-76, and Peikoff, *OPAR*, 12-14, 74-75.

17. In *ITOE*, Ayn Rand distinguishes between the axiomatic *concepts* of existence, consciousness, and identity, and the propositional form in which the axioms themselves are stated; and she discusses the respective cognitive roles of axiomatic concepts and propositional axioms. (*ITOE*, 55-61, 256-63.) It is worth mentioning that she certainly does not hold that all human knowledge is *deduced*, rationalist-style, from these axioms. In Aristotle's language, she holds that these axioms are, in effect, that *by which* we reason, not that *from which* we do. Reason operates, directly or indirectly, only on sensory-perceptual data, as we shall see in a later chapter.

18. One way that Ayn Rand's heroes and villains in *Atlas Shrugged* are shown to differ from each other is precisely with regard to their respective acceptances of, or attempts to evade, these axioms. See, e.g., in Galt's speech, 1015-18 (and passim), pb 933-36; *FTNI* 152-57, pb 124-28; and n. 3 in the next chapter.

5
Metaphysics
(continued)

Identity and Causality

What exist are entities with identity. To have identity is to be definite, determinate, specific. It is to have specific attributes—and not others. And it is to act in specific ways—and not others. The way an entity acts is part of what it is. But actions (or "events") are not separable and self-subsistent—they are merely what entities *do*, and they are consequent upon the actual attributes of those entities. On a level table, a ball, when pushed a little above its center point, rolls. A cube slides. What a thing can do, depends on what it is. And so Ayn Rand writes:

> The law of causality is the law of identity applied to action. All actions are caused by entities. The nature of an action is caused and determined by the nature of the entities that act; a thing cannot act in contradiction to its nature . . .
>
> The law of identity does not permit you to have your cake and eat it, too. The law of causality does not permit you to eat your cake *before* you have it.[1]

Outside agents often precipitate a thing's action—one billiard ball striking another results in the other billiard ball's action. But the second billiard ball's action is at least as much a function of its *own* identity; were it made of soft butter, the reaction would be different. Living organisms store their own energy and have a much more complicated repertoire of action in response to a given stimulus; the possession of consciousness allows an even greater repertoire. Man's consciousness, Ayn Rand maintains, is volitional and (as we will see in our chapter on man's nature) can initiate actions which are *caused* by the human agent himself, although they are not necessitated by antecedent conditions. The types of causation are many, but in all cases the primary locus of causation is in the nature—the inherent attributes —of the acting entity. [2]

The pervasiveness of attempts to deny or reverse causality—in morality, economics, and sex—is an important theme of *Atlas Shrugged*.[3] A deep respect for the principle of causality is a hallmark of an Ayn Rand hero.

The primacy of existence

We have seen that the primacy of existence is implicit in the axioms of existence and consciousness. It is also implicit in the axiom of identity. To say that *things are what they are* is to say that they are what they are *independent of consciousness*.

The contrasting orientation—the primacy of consciousness—can take various forms, depending on whether the consciousness given primacy is individual (as in radical forms of subjectivism), collective (either man's consciousness universally, or that of some social group), or "divine", or some combination thereof.[4]

Ayn Rand considers the contrast between the primacy of existence and the primacy of consciousness to be "the basic metaphysical issue that lies at the root of any system of philosophy,"[5] with implications for virtually every issue in philosophy.

Whether one gives metaphysical primacy to existence or consciousness shapes, for example, one's view of the relation between mind and body, and of whether the "supernatural" is possible, as we will see momentarily. In epistemology, she holds, it shapes one's view of what knowledge is and whether it is to be acquired by looking outward (via the senses to the world) or inward (to mental contents or to revelations from a supposed divine source). In ethics, it shapes one's view of the nature of values and how they are to be identified (by looking to man's nature and needs, or to mental contents such as desires, or to "divine revelation").

Whether one gives primacy to existence or consciousness also shapes one's basic mode of functioning throughout one's life, in regard both to the world and to other people, as Ayn Rand explained in a fascinating essay titled "The Metaphysical vs. the Man-Made" (1973). In this essay she discussed the relation between the primacy of existence and the Alcoholics Anonymous prayer, "God grant me the serenity to accept things I cannot change, courage to change things I can, and wisdom to know the difference." Rejecting the statement's theological content, she focused on its deeper philosophical significance.

She distinguished between "the metaphysically given"—those facts which are inherent in the nature of the universe such as scientific laws and events occurring outside of human control—and "the man-made"— "any object, institution, procedure, or rule of conduct made by man." She noted the frequency with which people rebel against the former and passively accept the latter, as if consciousness were metaphysically supreme and the basic nature of things malleable. On a primacy of existence orientation, she explained, "It is the metaphysically given that must be accepted: it cannot be changed. It is the man-made that must never be accepted uncritically: it must be judged, then accepted or rejected and changed when necessary."[6]

Mind and body

Ayn Rand's primacy of existence orientation is responsible for her distinctive view of the relation of mind and body. Various aspects of this view will be discussed as this book proceeds, but four basic ideas can be stated now. They are: (i) the existence of consciousness is axiomatic; (ii) consciousness is an attribute or action of (certain) living organisms; (iii) consciousness has causal efficacy; (iv) there is a fundamental harmony between mind and body.

First, as we have already observed, any denial of the existence of consciousness is self-refuting. Materialism, as a thesis that mind or consciousness either does not exist or is reducible to matter, cannot be sustained in any of its forms.

Second, consciousness cannot exist as a separate entity. Its connection to the body of a living organism is inescapable. Like anything else that exists, consciousness has identity. It operates by specific means, including sense organs, and expresses itself in bodily activity. We are directly aware of both of those facts in ourselves, and

46

our discovery of consciousness in others is an inference from their bodily activity. Only a view of consciousness (such as Descartes') that holds it to be self-contained epistemologically, with its own internal objects, could provide any support for the metaphysical independence of mind from body. But such a view violates the primacy of existence. Dualism, as a thesis that mind or consciousness is a distinct entity, cannot be sustained in any of its forms.

Third, that consciousness can direct action is evident. That it can do so in ourselves is evident to introspection; that it can do so in all other living entities that possess it is evident to observation. Indeed, in our chapter on man's nature we will see Ayn Rand's reasons for holding that the exercise of man's distinctive form of consciousness is non-deterministic and under his direct volitional control.[7]

(As for the precise relation between mind and brain, beyond the three propositions just mentioned, Ayn Rand held that that was a matter for science, not for philosophy.)

These three propositions, in the context of the primacy of existence orientation already discussed, support the fourth proposition—Ayn Rand's thesis of the fundamental harmony of mind and body.

To understand what is at stake we must recall the millennia-old insistence—from religious, philosophical, psychological, and literary quarters—on the fundamental conflicts of: soul vs. body, mind vs. heart, reason vs. the senses, the moral vs. the practical, love vs. sex, etc. The view that there is an inherent and fundamental war between different parts of man's nature, or different parts of his psyche, Ayn Rand called "the soul-body dichotomy". She commented on the pervasiveness of this view in western (and eastern) thought, from Plato (and before) to Christianity to secularized Christians such as Hobbes and Kant, on down through Freud to the present day.

We will discuss in due course her view of the proper relation and integration of each of these allegedly conflicting pairs. But it can be said at this point why she held in general that on the primacy of existence orientation there can be no such fundamental conflicts.

The element of truth in these dichotomies is the fact that conflicts do occur: man is neither omniscient nor infallible. Opposing ideas can both seem attractive. Reason and emotion can pull in opposite directions. One can experience opposing desires. But the interpretation of these conflicts is shaped by one's metaphysics.

If one is a metaphysical dualist and believes that there are two "realities" of opposing natures —a higher spiritual and a lower material world—one will tend to see man as a being of both worlds, and will

47

interpret such conflicts as signs of that same metaphysical war being waged within the human soul. As we have noted, though, metaphysical dualism is a product of the primacy of consciousness in one form or another. To someone on the primacy of existence orientation, who thus rejects metaphysical dualism, these conflicts will be seen rather as problems to be solved.

First, there is only one reality, the one man perceives, not two conflicting ones. And second, if consciousness is fundamentally *awareness* and not creation, then its products are the causal result of interactions between conscious organisms and reality. There will be, therefore, no innate content to consciousness—neither ideas nor desires nor irrational urges, destructive or otherwise. All conscious content will be the product of reason making identifications (whether logically or not) based on the direct awareness of reality provided by the senses, and then evaluating what it identifies according to some standard of value it has adopted (whether logically or not). Emotions and desires will be products of those evaluations. Conflicts will be the result of contradictory judgments—failures of integration—which subsequent thought (sometimes long and difficult) can in principle always correct.

This approach of Ayn Rand's, only sketched here, will take on increasing richness as we have occasion to explore, in subsequent chapters, each of the allegedly conflicting pairs. I venture to suggest in advance: (i) that there is no thinker in the history of philosophy who has as profoundly developed and integrated a view of the harmony of mind and body as has Ayn Rand, and (ii) that this is a consequence of the consistency and completeness of her acceptance of the primacy of existence orientation.

The "supernatural"

Both the concept of a "God" and the arguments traditionally offered for the existence of such a Being involve fundamental violations of the three axioms. Let's look first at the two most popular arguments.

The "first cause" (or "cosmological") argument maintains that God is needed as the creator or sustainer of the material universe. But that is to say that existence needs consciousness to create or sustain it. It makes a consciousness—God's consciousness—metaphysically prior to existence. But existence exists. It can have no beginning, no end, no cause. It just *is*. And consciousness is a faculty of awareness, not of

48

creation. The first cause argument violates both the axiom of existence and the axiom of consciousness.

The "design" (or "teleological") argument maintains that the highly complex order and organization in the world (e.g., in living things) could not have come about by chance. It must have come about by design and so needs a designer. But there is a third alternative: *nature* (i.e., identity). Things in the world come to be *by nature*—by the natures of the individual acting entities. (Chance is not an alternative to nature—it is just the beneficent or harmful interaction of independent causal chains.) If complex entities and relationships have come into being, then the natures of the entities whose interaction produced them were sufficient to produce them. It is sheer invention (i.e., the primacy of consciousness) to assume, in those cases where complexity has come into being, that the material nature of things is insufficient to generate it. (*How* such complexity arose is a matter for *science*, not philosophy. But that it *can* arise in nature is a consequence of the philosophic axiom of identity.)

Other arguments for the existence of God suffer a similar fate. God is not needed for morality: basic facts about man's nature as a rational living being are sufficient to generate an objective code of moral values, as we will see in our chapter on the foundations of ethics. Nor is God needed to ensure that the good will triumph in the end; indeed, the good as defined by religious traditions will not. But, armed with a proper metaphysics and epistemology, and a rational ethical code on which they act, men will find this already a "benevolent universe", in which the good does succeed. (In any case, *wanting* morality to be objective, or the good to succeed, is not an argument for the existence of a Being who might provide it. Things are what they are, and wishing, we may remind those tempted by such "arguments", does not make anything so.)

It is not only that there are no good arguments for the existence of God, Ayn Rand held. The very concept of "God" violates the axioms as well. "Omnipotence", "omniscience", and "infinity" (as used for God) all violate *identity*. That God knows, and acts, without means violates *causality*. And so on. Most fundamental of all, to postulate a God as creator of the universe is to postulate a consciousness that could exist without anything to be conscious of. This, as we have seen, violates *existence* and *consciousness*. "[A] consciousness with nothing to be conscious of is a contradiction in terms. A consciousness conscious of nothing but itself is a contradiction in terms: before it could identify itself as consciousness, it had to be conscious of something."[8] Existence *precedes* consciousness. Existence can, again, have no beginning, no end, no cause. It just . . . *exists.*[9]

The domain of metaphysics

In her journal notes, under the heading *"'Cosmology' has to be thrown out of philosophy,"* Ayn Rand observes that the history of metaphysics is filled with misguided attempts to deduce the nature of the universe—either from the currently latest stage of scientific discovery or from what would have to be the case about the world for some erroneous epistemological theory to be true. "Aristotle," she comments, "established the right metaphysics by establishing the law of identity—which was all that was necessary (plus the identification of the fact that only concretes exist). But he destroyed his metaphysics by his cosmology—by the whole nonsense of the 'moving spheres', 'the immovable mover', teleology, etc." Then she goes on:

> The real crux of the issue is that *philosophy is primarily epistemology*—the science of the means, the rules and the methods of human knowledge. Epistemology is the base of all other sciences and one necessary for man because man is a being of volitional consciousness—a being who has to discover, not only the content of his knowledge, but also the means by which he is to acquire knowledge. Observe that all philosophers (except Aristotle) have been projecting their epistemologies into their metaphysics (or that their metaphysics were merely epistemological and psychological confessions). All the fantastic irrationalities of philosophical metaphysics have been the result of epistemological errors, fallacies or corruptions. "Existence exists" (or identity plus causality) is all there is to metaphysics. *All the rest is epistemology.* [10]

"Existence exists" (or identity plus causality) has been the subject of this and the previous chapter. Ayn Rand's epistemology will be the subject of the next two.

Endnotes

1. *AS*, 1037, pb 954; *FTNI*, 188, pb 151.
2. For a fuller presentation, see Peikoff, *OPAR*, 12-17. The philosopher David Hume tried to argue against a view of causality like that of Ayn Rand's by claiming that there was no necessary connection between a thing's sensible attributes and its actions. But his argument rests on a host of philosophical theses that Ayn Rand rejects (as have other philosophers from Aristotle onward). These errors include Hume's distinction between "matters of fact" and "relations of ideas", and two of the views that underlie it: his "sensationalist" subjective empiricism and his "nominalist" theory of concepts. These epistemological errors give rise to numerous metaphysical errors (including his rejection of the Aristotelian concept of an entity and his subjectivist account of necessity). For the elements of Ayn Rand's reasons for rejecting these theses of Hume and their consequences for our understanding of causality, see *FTNI*, 29-30; the theory of concepts in *ITOE*; and Leonard Peikoff's "The Analytic-Synthetic Dichotomy", *ITOE*, 88-121. For more on the metaphysical issues surrounding causality, see *ITOE*, 264-306, and (on her view of necessity) *PWNI*, 28-41, pb 23-34, and Peikoff, *OPAR*, 23-28.
3. *AS*, 489, 1038, pb 455, 954; *FTNI*, 117-18, 189, pb 99, 152.
4. It was Ayn Rand's view that all "dualist" metaphysical systems that postulate a "higher" reality beyond the one we perceive were based on one or another form of the primacy of consciousness. We will see this for the theological version later in this chapter. For the way in which this is true for Platonism, see *ITOE*, 53-54, and Peikoff, *OPAR*, 145-46.

     The social version of the primacy of consciousness is prevalent today under the name of "the social construction of reality". This view seems to have evolved out of the failure of the universalist version, which was introduced by Kant, via a tradition from Hegel through the pragmatists (and others) to the present day.

     The individual version of the primacy of consciousness is implicit in the common remark that "everyone has his own reality", but people who say that often are focused on the fact that

51

people's *beliefs* about reality sometimes differ, and that people's actions are shaped by their beliefs. But it is all-important to recognize that, although there may be different sets of beliefs, there is only one *reality*—and that we each should seek to have our beliefs conform to it. If one truly denies this, then one *is* endorsing the primacy of consciousness in its stark individual version.

Unstable mixtures of the primacy of existence and the primacy of consciousness orientations have also been maintained, but they *are* unstable, and tend to collapse into a more consistent primacy of consciousness orientation. (See the previous chapter, note 12, for a famous example.)

5. *PWNI*, 29; pb 24.
6   *PWNI*, ch. 3. For further discussion, see Peikoff, *OPAR*, 17-30. Peikoff discusses many more aspects and implications of the primacy of existence and primacy of consciousness orientations; and he presents Ayn Rand's view of the *order* in which a human being grasps the axioms and corollaries we have discussed.
7. Ayn Rand thus rejects epiphenomenalism as well as materialism and dualism.
8. Above, p. 38.
9 . At this point theists often assert that God is beyond man's power to understand. But so is nonsense. If something exists, it has identity. If it has identity, it can, in principle, be understood. There is a fascinating discussion in Galt's speech of the psychological issues involved here, both in those who would surrender their minds in this way and in those who demand that surrender (*AS*, 1044-46, pb 960-62; *FTNI*, 200-203, pb 160-62).
10. *Journals*, 699. She does not mean, of course, to exclude ethics and the other branches of philosophy. They are the application of metaphysics and epistemology to man's life—the "technology" to the "theoretical foundation" of philosophy that is metaphysics and epistemology (*PWNI*, 3).

6

Perception and Concepts

Our need of epistemology

Let us look again at the opening of Ayn Rand's journal entry quoted at the end of the previous chapter.

> The real crux of the issue is that *philosophy is primarily epistemology*—the science of the means, the rules, and the methods of human knowledge. Epistemology is the base of all other sciences and one necessary for man because man is a being of volitional consciousness—a being who has to discover, not only the content of his knowledge, but also the means by which he is to acquire knowledge.

This argument rests ultimately on the primacy of existence. Since the mind does not create what exists, it can know what exists only if it follows processes that ensure that its content derives from and conforms to what exists.

But the exercise of our minds is not automatic. We need to *direct* our minds to the goal of knowledge and to the processes that actually achieve that goal. And we can make errors. We need "rules for the direction of the mind."[1] Indeed, for the full range of knowledge necessary for the achievement and enjoyment of life, man needs a fully articulated understanding of "the means, the rules, and the methods of human knowledge." Epistemology is the science devoted to achieving that understanding—and our need of it is central to our existence.

Much of the history of epistemology, Ayn Rand argues in the title essay of *For the New Intellectual*, is a history of failures—and of

53

claims that man is unable to achieve objective knowledge of independent reality. Twentieth century philosophy in particular has been permeated with skepticism and this has infected much of the century's history and culture. In fact, as she shows in that essay, the dominant epistemology of an era has always been a major determinant of its prevailing culture. Ayn Rand's aim in her epistemology is to vindicate man's mind—to show its efficacy and power. The widespread acceptance of her epistemological theory would produce a cultural revolution.

Sense perception

Sense perception, according to Ayn Rand, is our primary form of awareness, on which the conceptual level builds. It is thus a *direct* awareness of what exists—of entities, including their attributes, relations, and actions. The validity of the senses—i.e., the fact that the senses provide us with direct awareness of independent objects—is thus *axiomatic*, according to Ayn Rand. We are *directly* aware of individual people, trees, cars, desks; their shapes, colors, and positions relative to each other; their movements and sounds they make; and so on.

It is no accident, then, that this is the "common sense" position and that all philosophers who deny it have started by raising objections to this common sense view. They claim that "what we actually see" does not match what we know of the entities we are "supposed" to be seeing. The senses, they say, "distort" reality (and "deceive" us); what we are directly aware of, they conclude, are not material entities but inner objects from which we are to infer to (or, worse, construct) the real. All such views, Ayn Rand holds, are in the end self-refuting, and are based on an erroneous view either of the role of sense perception in knowledge or of the nature of direct conscious awareness as such.[2]

The self-refuting character of all claims that the senses "distort" reality and "deceive" us is evident in the standard examples offered of this.

"The senses tell us that railroad tracks converge in the distance," it is said, "and yet we know that they don't." But how do we know that? We go down and . . . *look*.

"Our senses tell us that the stick in water is bent," it is said, "and yet we know that it's not." But how do we know that? We reach in and . . . *feel*. We take it out and . . . *look*.

The senses do not "deceive" us, Ayn Rand explains, because they do not *interpret* the world at all. Interpretation is done by the mind—

by reason operating with concepts. Perceptual awareness is the inexorable result of a causal interaction between physical entities and physical sense organs (and the nervous system and brain). This awareness may lead, on the conceptual level, to mistaken judgments about what we perceive. But the very same perceptual awareness provides us with the means to correct our judgments and expand our knowledge of the world—and these corrections come early in life.

We quickly learn as children to differentiate between the look of parallel railroad tracks in the distance and how they would look if they actually converged. And the look parallel tracks have is what allows us to determine distance. A child is fooled once when seeing a straight stick in water, but soon learns (pre-conceptually) to see it as straight. And the similarity of the look of a straight stick in water to the look of a bent stick in air teaches us, at the conceptual level, about *refraction*. And so on.

> The task of [man's] senses is to give him the evidence of existence, but the task of identifying it belongs to his reason, his senses tell him only that something *is*, but *what* it is must be learned by his mind.[3]

The deeper issue behind the failure to recognize that sensory-perceptual awareness is a direct awareness of physical entities has to do with the very nature of consciousness. Philosophers assume that if we are to be "directly" aware of something, our consciousness must be completely passive—it must "mirror" what it is aware of. They then observe that our perception of physical entities requires a causal interaction between those entities and our sense organs, nervous system, and brain. What we are aware of, they conclude, is the effect within consciousness of that interaction—mental contents ("sense data"), not the physical entities that initiate the causal chain.

Ayn Rand accepts the initial datum—that perceptual *awareness* is the result of an interaction between physical entities and a physical sensory apparatus. But she rejects the conclusion that what we are aware *of* is only effects within consciousness. And she rejects it because she rejects the premise that direct awareness must be passive and mirror-like. Instead she introduces a distinction between the *form* of perception and the *object* of perception.

Like everything else, consciousness too *has identity*, she observes. Consciousness is an attribute or action of a living organism. It operates *by specific means* and *in a specific form*. Awareness of entities (including their attributes) is the result of a physical interaction, but that

55

result *is* a direct awareness *of* those entities (including their attributes). The form in which we perceive a rectangular envelope when tilted relative to our line of sight, for example, is partly determined by the envelope's rectangularity and partly determined by the angle of our line of sight (and certain properties of our eyes). But as perceivers focused on the object (and not, introspectively, on the form per se), we have no trouble seeing the rectangular object as rectangular, either from that angle or as we move around the object.

We can go further. Even were our sense organs different, though still responsive to the same attribute of an object, the *form* in which we perceive that attribute would be different, but *what* we perceive would be the same. Let's illustrate this with a fanciful example.

Imagine an extraterrestrial being who perceived the world in the form not of color but of musical tones. That is to say, suppose that as his "eyes" (i.e., light receptors) scanned a room and detected different wavelengths of light, he had experiences much like what we experience when we hear different musical tones. (We are assuming he responds to the same range of visible light and can discriminate roughly the same differences between wavelengths.) Where we perceive the color, say, of the leaves of a plant as green, he experiences something like what we would experience when hearing, say, middle C on the piano.

Ayn Rand's view is that the extraterrestrial would be perceiving the same entities, and the same attributes of those entities, as we do, although in a different form. But this has no philosophical significance. Where we perceive similarities between objects, he would perceive similarities. Where we have the basis for forming certain concepts, he would have the basis for forming the same concepts. Nothing would prevent him from arriving at the same physical theories that we do.

We may ask two questions. First, what is that same attribute we are both perceiving, albeit in different forms? Second, what is the metaphysical status of the different forms of perception? Let's start with the second question. In the human case, what is the metaphysical status of the green we experience?

Traditionally we are offered two alternatives: the form in which we perceived the green color is either "in the object" or it is "in the mind". The correct answer, Ayn Rand says, is *neither*. The form in which we perceive the color of the plant is, as we have seen, the result of a physical interaction. As such it cannot be located in either of the interacting objects. (When two cars collide, Ayn Rand asks, in which car is the collision? Obviously neither, since it is an *inter*action.). And it is certainly not "in the mind", since the green is the form in which we perceive the color *of the plant*.

56

That takes us to our first question. What is that same attribute that is perceived in two different forms? Well, says Ayn Rand, it is the green color. It is the object's being of such a nature that it will be perceived by humans in this form and by the extraterrestrials in that form. This is a single property or attribute of the object, identified relationally—it's what we call its *green color*. Scientific (not philosophic) study allows us to identify the underlying causal basis of this property —*what* that nature is. The object's green color is not to be simply identified with that underlying causal basis, since the latter is inherent in the object, and the former is an inherent property qua interacting a certain way with conscious organisms. But both are real. And although the underlying causal basis has to be inferred, the green color of the object is something we are *directly* aware of, though in a certain form.[4]

Perceptual awareness is, then, direct awareness of the world. All of man's knowledge begins with perception, and perception is the ultimate test of all of his conclusions. But perceptual awareness is only the beginning of human knowledge. Man's distinctive method of cognition is to integrate his percepts into *concepts* and to understand the world in conceptual form.[5]

Concepts

Ayn Rand's theory of concepts is the most complex aspect of her philosophy. It cannot be adequately summarized in the space available here. My aim is to introduce some of the highlights of the theory in order to provide both sufficient basis for what follows and sufficient stimulus, I hope, for readers to pursue its study further.[6]

Concepts expand the range of our awareness beyond the perceptual to things inaccessible to the senses, either because they are too far in space or time, too large or small in size, too many in number, too subtly different, too remotely similar (and so on). They allow a grasp of all things of a kind—past, present, and future. And perhaps most important, they allow specialized study: by studying some members of a conceptualized group, we are able to learn about all the members of that group. All of science and technology rest on this fact.

Ayn Rand asks how that is possible. Is the grouping which concepts permit an invention of our minds or does it have a basis in fact? "[T]he validity of man's knowledge depends on the validity of concepts. But concepts are abstractions or universals, and everything that man perceives is particular, concrete. What is the relationship between abstractions and concretes? To what precisely do concepts refer in reality? . . . Where is the 'manness' in men? What, in reality, corresponds to the concept 'man' in our mind?"

Traditional "realist" theories have held that concepts have distinct, "abstract" objects of their own, different from the objects of which we are aware. Ayn Rand denies this. Concepts are integrations of perceptual data. They are a distinctive form of awareness of the very same kinds of individual items available to perception.

Understanding the process of concept-formation will be central to understanding what concepts are, so Ayn Rand begins by tracing the process by which concepts are formed. She then asks what metaphysical facts underlie the process. A revolutionary dimension of her theory is her view that these facts are fundamentally mathematical in nature.

The formation of concepts is based on a grasp of similarity among the existents being conceptualized. Ayn Rand gives examples across the full range of concepts; we will here restrict ourselves to her first two examples, "length" and, especially, "table".

The grasp of similarity begins at the perceptual level. By the time we first notice similarity, we have long been aware that something exists, and we are perceptually discriminating entities from their background. We recognize these entities as specific, individual things and distinguish them from each other. In time we begin to notice (still wordlessly) that some entities (e.g., two tables) are like each other and different from some other entity or entities (e.g., a chair). (Similarity is always and only recognized against a background of difference.)

The next step, Ayn Rand holds, is key. It is the grouping of objects according to their similarities, regarding each of them as a "*unit*"—i.e., as "a separate member of a group of two or more similar members". The child's mind "is focusing on a particular attribute of the objects (their shape), then isolating them according to their differences, and integrating them as units into separate groups according to their similarities."

> This is the key, the entrance to the conceptual level of man's consciousness. The ability to regard entities as units is man's distinctive method of cognition . . .

To step through to the conceptual level—to form his first concept —the child must *integrate* that grouping of units into a single new mental entity, a unitary awareness of that group. "A concept," Ayn

Rand defines, "is a mental integration of two or more units which are isolated according to a specific characteristic(s) and united by a specific definition."

The isolation is a separating out (e.g., of the tables from the chairs). The uniting is the integration, the production of a new mental entity—a unitary awareness of the group. So that the integration may be retained, it is designated by a perceptual concrete—a word. The concept is fixed (i.e., given precise identity) by a definition. (At the earliest stages, the "definition" might be the sort of image reflected in children's stick-figure drawings; but later the definition will need to be verbal as we will discuss in the next chapter.)

This, Ayn Rand says, is "a general description of the nature of concepts as products of a certain mental process. But *the* question of epistemology is: what precisely is the nature of that process? To what precisely do concepts refer in reality?"

The key is to identify the metaphysical basis of similarity, using certain concepts from mathematics. "The process of concept-formation is in large part a mathematical process." The central idea is that of *measurement*—"the identification of a quantitative relationship established by means of a standard that serves as a unit."

Measurement is a way of making the quantitative dimension of any attribute understandable by relating it to an easily perceivable unit of that attribute. E.g., the length of a certain hallway (or the distance to the moon) can be grasped with precision by relating it quantitatively to a standard *length* of one-foot or one-meter. Likewise, weights are measured by a unit weight, angle sizes by a unit angle size, etc. More complex attributes (e.g., shape), and entities themselves (e.g., tables) can be measured by measuring their simpler attributes.

The grasp of similarity is not an inexplicable, subjective phenomenon. Similarity is an implicit form of measurement, and the quantitative relationship it identifies is the factual basis both making possible and justifying the integration of similar existents into a concept. "Similarity, in this context, is the relationship between two or more existents which possess the same characteristic(s), but in different measure or degree."

In forming the concept "table", for example:

> The child's mind isolates two or more tables from other objects, by focusing on their distinctive characteristic: their shape. He observes that their shapes vary, but have one characteristic in common: a flat, level surface and support(s). He

59

forms the concept "table" by retaining that characteristic and omitting *all* particular measurements, not only the measurements of the shape, but of all the other characteristics of tables (many of which he is not aware of at the time).[7]

The measurements omitted (which we, as adults, could specify in much more detail) are not regarded as non-existent. "The principle is: the relevant measurements must exist in *some* quantity, but may exist in *any* quantity." The child is not explicitly aware of establishing quantitative relationships among the objects he integrates into a concept —he merely perceives their similarity. But the commensurability relationships that we have mentioned (and that Ayn Rand discusses in much more detail) are necessary both for the concept to be formed and for the grouping it represents to have a basis in reality.

"*A concept*," Ayn Rand defines, expanding her initial characterization, "*is a mental integration of two or more units possessing the same distinguishing characteristic(s), with their particular measurements omitted.*"

What, then, is the "manness" in men? It is not some identical essence running through all individual men (more on essence in the next chapter); nor is it an arbitrary grouping based on some vague, unanalyzable resemblance. It is the possession of a large set of distinguishing characteristics (some known, some not yet known) in varying measure or degree—on the understanding that they must exist in some quantity, but may exist in any quantity (within the range permitted by those characteristics).

Consider a simpler example, three objects each possessing length: a pen 5 inches long, a ruler 12 inches long, and a hallway 10 feet (120 inches) long. Their common length is not, for Ayn Rand, a matter of their each possessing some identical abstract attribute, "length" (to which is "contingently" added "5 inches", "12 inches", "120 inches"). Nor is it a matter of their each possessing different but irreducibly similar attributes "being five inches long", "being 12 inches long", "being 120 inches long". It is a matter of their each being "*x inches long*".

They each possess the same attribute (length) but in varying measure or degree. No attribute can exist without existing in some particular measure or degree, but the concept, while recognizing that fact, omits the specification of that measure or degree, and thus unites the many individuals into one mental unit by which they are grasped and understood.

Everything we have discussed in this section is from the first two chapters of *Introduction to Objectivist Epistemology*. In subsequent chapters, Ayn Rand applies this theory to the full range of concepts, including "abstractions from abstractions" (i.e., integrations and subdivisions of previously formed concepts), the many different types of concepts of consciousness (where a different kind of measurement is involved), and (after a chapter on definitions) axiomatic concepts.

She goes on, in a chapter titled "The Cognitive Role of Concepts", to discuss the fact that consciousness, at any level, can work only with a small number of units at one time. This fact gives rise to what Ayn Rand calls "the principle of unit-economy", which explains many features of conceptual functioning and provides guidelines for the correct use of concepts. She uses this principle to identify when the formation of a new concept is mandatory, when it is cognitively inappropriate, and when it is optional; she then uses these rules to discuss the notorious "borderline case problem".

In the chapter on definition, she introduces her views that (i) essences are "epistemological" and not "metaphysical", and (ii) concepts and essences are *objective*, a status she distinguishes from "intrinsic" and "subjective". In a final chapter titled "Consciousness and Identity", she steps back to discuss the theoretical basis for this concept of objectivity. To complete our introduction to Ayn Rand's theory of concepts, and to her epistemology, we turn to her view of definition and essence, her thesis that concepts are objective, and her general view of the nature of objectivity.

Endnotes

1. I borrow this elegant phrase from Descartes, notwithstanding his failure to grasp the primacy of existence, on which such rules actually depend. (See above, p. 39 with n. 12.) The second thesis just mentioned on which our need of epistemology depends—that the action of man's consciousness (above the sensory-perceptual level) is initiated and directed *volitionally*—could well be discus-

61

sed in this context (as it is by Leonard Peikoff, in *OPAR*, ch. 2) since it is a precondition of epistemology. However, we will save it for our chapter on Ayn Rand's general view of man's nature and simply presume it for now.

2. This is not to say that the metaphysical thesis of the primacy of existence *derives from* a certain epistemology. The primacy of existence, Ayn Rand holds, is axiomatic. It is self-evident in perceptual awareness that what we are directly aware of is independent of our consciousness. But its status as self-evident can be hidden from someone who is confused by an erroneous epistemological theory. Ayn Rand's discussion of the axiomatic validity of the senses aims to remove any such confusion, not to derive that axiomatic validity from anything more basic.

3. *AS*, 1016, pb 934; *FTNI*, 153, pb 125. See also *AS*, 1041, pb 957; *FTNI*, 193, pb 155.

4. For further discussion and for other aspects of Ayn Rand's theory of perception, including her rejection of the primary-secondary quality distinction, see *ITOE*, 279-82, and Peikoff, *OPAR*, 39-54.

5. Ayn Rand recognizes that the earliest stage or level of awareness is sensory, consisting of responses to individual stimuli, without discrimination of whole entities. The integration of sensations into percepts is done automatically by the brain. Our awareness of entities is direct, and not via conscious inference or "computation". All theories that claim that perception is, in effect, sensation plus concepts, rest, she holds, on faulty theories both of perception and of concepts. They reflect a failure to understand that perception is a form of awareness distinct from both sensation and conceptual awareness; and that concepts are formed *from* perceptual data and therefore cannot exist (in any form, not even as "schematisms") prior to perception.

6. The theory is presented in *ITOE*, and is summarized in Peikoff, *OPAR*, chs. 3 and 4. All subsequent quotations in this chapter come from the first two chapters of *ITOE*.

7. Notice that the distinguishing characteristic of tables, a certain type of shape, itself represents a range of measurements within a commensurable characteristic (viz., *shape*) shared by the objects from which tables are differentiated. This will prove especially important when we come to definitions in the next chapter.

7
Objectivity

Definitions

In the formation of a concept, as we have seen, the units (e.g., tables) are first *isolated* from certain other objects (e.g., chairs, beds) by focusing on a distinguishing characteristic(s) (e.g., a specific shape, and, later, a use). Then the units are *integrated* by retaining that characteristic(s) while omitting all particular measurements (of that shape, and that use, and of all the other characteristics of tables). The integration is turned into a manageable unit by being assigned a word. To complete the process the concept is given a *definition*.

"A definition," says Ayn Rand, "is a statement that identifies the nature of the units subsumed under a concept. . . . The purpose of a definition is to distinguish a concept from all other concepts and thus to keep its units differentiated [in one's mind] from all other existents."[1]

> The rules of correct definition are derived from the process of concept-formation. . . . A definition . . . specifies the distinguishing characteristic(s) of the units, and indicates the category of existents from which they were differentiated.
>
> The distinguishing characteristic(s) of the units becomes the *differentia* of the concept's definition; the existents possessing [the shared commensurable characteristic] become the *genus*.
>
> Thus a definition complies with the two essential functions of consciousness: differentiation and integration. The differentia isolates the units of a concept from all other existents; the genus indicates their connection to a wider group of existents.[2]

The units of a concept normally have many distinguishing characteristics, however, and to specify them all in its definition would defeat the purpose of a definition—it would make it impossible for a mind to hold the concept as a single unit, clearly grasped. The differentia, therefore, must be restricted to the *essential* characteristic(s), i.e., the characteristic(s) that constitutes the basic nature of the units under the concept—i.e., the characteristic(s) that, as the source of the others, condenses and implies them.[3] Here Ayn Rand adopts Aristotle's *rule of fundamentality*. The essential characteristic is the *fundamental* one —i.e., the characteristic that is *responsible for* (and thus explains) the greatest number of others.

Two facts about this process will have significant implications, says Ayn Rand. First, a concept is an integration of existents, not just of selected aspects of them, so that the meaning of a concept is not exhausted by its definition. Second, knowledge about the units of a concept is acquired over time, and new knowledge may require a revised definition. Both facts are best seen in the context of Ayn Rand's general approach to concepts, as presented in the previous chapter.

A concept is an integration of perceptual data. It is not an awareness of special "abstract" objects, but a distinct and powerful form of awareness of particular existents—past, present and future, known and unknown—with all their attributes, known and unknown. The concept is formed by a certain *means* (isolation and integration via measurement-omission) and in a certain *form* (an integration of retained characteristics with measurement omitted, held by a word and specified by a definition). But neither the means by which conceptual awareness of existents is achieved, nor the form in which is it is held, is the *object* of conceptual awareness. The object is the units, the *existents* grouped together, with all of their attributes.

The concept's content is thus not to be equated with its definition. As one comes to discover additional distinguishing characteristics of the units of a concept, one's knowledge of those units changes—it expands. But *one's concept does not change*. The concept still integrates the very same units, i.e., the very same existents.[4]

However, if one should discover a more fundamental distinguishing characteristic of the existents integrated into a concept, the definition will need to change to reflect that new knowledge. In the new context of knowledge, the old defining characteristic is no longer essential, and falls out of the definition. The earlier definition is still a true statement, and the earlier essential characteristic (and its causal relationship to the other earlier known distinguishing characteristics) is still included in the content of the concept, but it is replaced in the definition. Our knowledge has *expanded*, and our definition reflects that.[5]

The essential characteristic of a concept, then, is that distinguishing characteristic of its units, *from among those known*, which is responsible for (and thus explains) the greatest number of other *known* distinguishing characteristics.

Definitions are thus *contextual*. They depend in part on the definer's context of knowledge. But within a given context of knowledge they are "*absolute*"—i.e., determined by the *actual* causal relationships between the distinguishing characteristics known within that context. "An objective definition, valid for all men," Ayn Rand says, "is one that designates the *essential* distinguishing characteristic(s) and genus of the existents subsumed under a given concept—according to all the relevant knowledge available at that stage of mankind's development."[6]

Definitions are also *factual statements*. "A definition is a condensation of a vast body of observations"[7]—of similarity-and-difference-relationships, of which characteristics distinguish a group of existents from others, and of which of those characteristic(s) are in fact responsible for the rest. They are neither "stipulations" nor "conventions".

Because concepts are based in perceptual data, and reflect the proper differentiation and integration of that data, we have a method of resolving uncertainty about the precise meaning or definition of a concept. "[T]he best method of clarification," Ayn Rand writes, "is to look for [the concept's] referents—i.e., to ask oneself: What fact or facts of reality gave rise to this concept? What distinguishes it from all other concepts?" We have already seen this method at work in several places in Ayn Rand's thought, and will see it again later in her analysis of the foundation of ethics.[8]

Concepts as objective

If definitions are contextual for Ayn Rand, so are essences. Or, as she put it, essences are *epistemological*, not metaphysical. A distinguishing characteristic that is causally prior to other distinguishing characteristics is not for that reason more "real" than those other characteristics, nor more what an existent integrated by the concept "really is", nor is it the sole referent of the concept. The concept refers to the existents it integrates, including all of their characteristics, known and unknown. But the characteristic designated "essential" does perform a distinct *epistemological* function. This function depends in part on the factual (causal) relations between the characteristics, but in part on the way a conceptual consciousness must function if it is to acquire, retain, and expand its knowledge.

This feature of essential characteristics—that they are "a device of man's method of cognition"—points to a general feature of concepts as such. They too are "a device of man's method of cognition." They are not passive gazes at abstract entities, "universals", existing as such independent of the mind (as the "realist" tradition has held). Nor are they products of man's consciousness, unrelated to the facts of reality (as the "nominalist" tradition has held). Concepts, that is to say, are neither *intrinsic* nor *subjective*— they are *objective*,

> i.e., neither revealed nor invented, but . . . produced by man's consciousness in accordance with the facts of reality, as mental integrations of factual data computed by man—as the products of a cognitive method of classification whose processes must be performed by man, but whose content is dictated by reality.[9]

The nature of objectivity

In the Introduction we spoke of the centrality to Ayn Rand's thought of her concept of objectivity, noting its application in metaphysics (reality is objective), in epistemology (knowledge is objective), and in ethics (values are objective). We can now see why she held that the *epistemological* objectivity is the central concept.

To speak of reality as "objective" is to assert the primacy of existence. This may be useful in distinguishing one's position from any form of the primacy of consciousness, but strictly the term is superfluous. Reality isn't "objective"—it just is.

In epistemology, however, i.e., in man's cognitive functioning, there is a basic choice that gives rise to the need for a concept of the objective. Man may choose to function via a method that respects both the facts of reality and the nature of his consciousness, or he may not. However, if he is to succeed in acquiring knowledge, he must discover what that method is, and must choose to follow it.[10] (Objectivity in ethics, we will see later, is an application of the concept as it is used in epistemology.)

Notice both the parallels between the conceptual and perceptual levels, according to Ayn Rand, and their important differences.

In both cases the basic facts are the same. Consciousness has identity. We are aware *by a certain means* and *in a certain form*.

At the perceptual level, we are aware of entities (including their attributes). The *means* of awareness in perception is physiological—the brain integrates the data provided by sensory contact with these entities. The result is a perceptual *form* of direct awareness of these entities (including their attributes).

At the conceptual level, we are aware of entities (including their attributes), and can grasp any aspect of any existent, both within and outside the range of perceptual awareness. The *means* is the *process* of concept-formation—the isolation and integration of perceptual data, the formulating of definitions (and every other cognitive process that builds on concepts). The *form* of awareness is the *concept*—the integrated grasp of particulars possessing the same distinguishing characteristics with their measurements omitted.

In both cases, the form of awareness is neither "out there" apart from the mind nor "in here" as a creation of the mind unrelated to reality. It is the result of an interaction. It is the form in which we are aware of *that which exists*. In these respects the perceptual and conceptual levels are the same.

They differ in that the perceptual level is automatic, while the conceptual level is not. It has to be directed, and it has to be directed volitionally. The means of conceptual awareness—the proper methods for acquiring knowledge—must be discovered, and we must choose to use them.

We may then, following Leonard Peikoff, define Ayn Rand's view of objectivity as follows: "To be 'objective' in one's conceptual activities is volitionally to adhere to reality by following certain rules of method, a method based on facts *and* appropriate to man's form of cognition.[11]

Some people (and philosophers) may be tempted to short-circuit that process. They may look for automatic answers, viewing knowledge as a passive gaze at "higher" objects, existing intrinsically and somehow revealed directly to us. Others may turn inward, constructing knowledge from subjective mental contents of one sort or another. We need to understand, though, that neither of these approaches will work, since existence is primary and consciousness has identity.[12] To conceptualize the proper alternative—viz., the commitment to process the fullest range of factual data according to methods dictated by the nature of human consciousness—we need the concept of *objectivity*. As Ayn Rand writes, in the concluding paragraphs of *Introduction to Objectivist Epistemology*:

> Objectivity begins with the realization that man (including his every attribute and faculty, including his consciousness) is an entity of a specific nature who must act accordingly; that there is no escape from the law of identity, neither in the universe with which he deals nor in the working of his own consciousness, and if he is to acquire knowledge of the first, he must discover the proper method of using the second; that there is no room for the *arbitrary* in any activity of man, least of all in his method of cognition—and just as he has learned to be guided by objective criteria in making his physical tools, so he must be guided by objective criteria in forming his tools of cognition: his concepts.
>
> Just as man's physical existence was liberated when he grasped the principle that "nature, to be commanded, must be obeyed," so his consciousness will be liberated when he grasps that *nature, to be apprehended, must be obeyed*—that the rules of cognition must be derived from the nature of existence and the nature, the *identity*, of his cognitive faculty.[13]

Endnotes

1. *ITOE*, 40. The only concepts which cannot "be defined and communicated in terms of other concepts . . . are concepts referring to sensations, and metaphysical axioms." These must be defined ostensively (40-41).
2. *ITOE*, 41. A definition thus both *differentiates* a concept from other concepts and *integrates* it to them, allowing us, as our knowledge expands, to retain the *hierarchy* of our concepts and to keep our knowledge integrated into a single whole.
3. Ayn Rand's use of "(s)" in referring to a concept's essential or fundamental "characteristic(s)" is her way of acknowledging that in certain kinds of existents two or more characteristics are *jointly* responsible for all or most of the remaining characteristics. To simplify the presentation in what follows, I will mostly omit the

"(s)", counting on readers to supply it where appropriate.

4. The concept itself will change—or, strictly, be replaced—only in those cases where new information, or a newly established scientific theory, so modifies our understanding of the similarity relationships as to require a reclassification of the relevant existents.

5. An example in the history of chemistry is the discovery of atomic number, based on the discovery of the internal structure of the atom and the role of the matched number of protons and electrons in determining many properties of atoms. Atoms had previously been defined in terms of atomic weight; the discovery of a more fundamental characteristic resulted in a change in the definition.

6. *ITOE*, 46.

7. *ITOE*, 48.

8. This description of the method, with an example, appears in *ITOE*, 51-52. The method was mentioned above, pp. 10, 22, and exhibited at work in her discussion of our need of philosophy in ch. 3.

9. *ITOE*, 54.

10. This is the root of the everyday injunction to "be objective". It is an injunction to attend to the facts, and process them rationally— i.e., in the way required if one is to *know* what one is talking about.

11. *OPAR*, 117.

12. In the history of thought, Ayn Rand observes, "The dichotomy of 'intrinsic or subjective' has played havoc with this issue [the nature of concepts] and with every issue involving the relationship of consciousness to existence." (*ITOE*, 53.)

13. *ITOE*, 82. The theory of concepts and of objectivity introduced in this and the preceding chapter have many implications that we cannot go into in this book. (Many of them are discussed in *OPAR*, chs. 4 and 5.) Ayn Rand's view that a concept is not to be equated with its definition (or with any subset of the characteristics of its units), and that definitions are factual, along with her view of causality and necessity, led her to a wholesale rejection of the traditional analytic-synthetic dichotomy. (See *ITOE*, 88-121.) It is perhaps clear already from what has been said about concepts and definitions (e.g. above, pp. 64, 65) that she would reject both the traditional Fregean view that "meaning determines reference" and the more recent "direct reference" theories. More generally, it would be her view that the treatment of all issues in the philosophy of language must be based on a proper theory of concepts.

8

Man: The Volitionally Rational Living Being

A philosophical concept of man

In the Introduction we spoke of Ayn Rand's heroic view of man. To view man as heroic one needs both a view of man's capacities and a standard of heroism. This chapter is concerned with the first of these—Ayn Rand's philosophical conception of man's nature and powers. The following chapter will examine the source and nature of an objective standard of moral value.

A philosophical view of man is built on metaphysics and epistemology. Previous chapters have introduced: man's existence and identity, his being subject to causality (properly understood), the relation of his consciousness to existence, and the operation of his basic cognitive faculties, viz., sense perception and concepts.[1]

To these metaphysical and epistemological fundamentals regarding man Ayn Rand adds three basic propositions: (i) man is a living being; (ii) reason is man's means of survival; and (iii) the exercise of reason is volitional.

The volitional character of reason provides the basis for Ayn Rand's understanding both of the relation of reason and emotion and of man's metaphysical relation to other men.

A living being

To understand man, Ayn Rand holds, one must first understand what it is to be a living being—i.e., one must understand the nature of *life*.

The distinction between living and non-living is grasped very early in man's conceptual development and remains a fundamental distinction near the base of our conceptual hierarchy. The most evident difference between the living and the non-living, as Aristotle pointed out, is that of motion vs. stillness—more precisely, self-motion vs. the absence of self-motion.

Living things initiate movement. They grow, plants turn towards the sun, animals run, swim, crawl, fly—and there is ceaseless internal motion throughout every part of a living thing—something that becomes increasingly evident as our tools for investigating living things increase in power.

The action of living things is thus *self-generated*, Ayn Rand observes. It is also *self-sustaining*. The actions of living things are not random—they are goal-directed. That is to say, living things are built so as to take the actions necessary to keep themselves in existence.[2] "Life," Ayn Rand described, "is a process of self-sustaining and self-generated action".

Living things *need* to take self-sustaining action because they face a basic alternative: existence or non-existence. The continued existence of a living thing is *conditional upon its own action*.

> There is only one fundamental alternative in the universe: existence or non-existence—and it pertains to a single class of entities: to living organisms. The existence of inanimate matter is unconditional, the existence of life is not: it depends on a specific course of action. Matter is indestructible, it changes its forms, but it cannot cease to exist. It is only a living organism that faces a constant alternative: the issue of life or death. Life is a process of self-sustaining and self-generated action. If an organism fails in that action, it dies; its chemical elements remain, but its life goes out of existence.[3]

The actions necessary for the survival of a living organism depend on its nature—its particular constitution, its capacities for action, and the needs required to sustain that constitution and those capacities. The actions required will differ from species to species.[4] To understand any species one must understand its basic means of survival.

Reason as man's means of survival

"Consciousness—for those living organisms which possess it—is the basic means of survival. For man, the basic means of survival is reason."[5] This thesis about man is a central theme of *Atlas Shrugged*. Ayn Rand first stated it in this eloquent passage in *The Fountainhead*:

> Man cannot survive except through his mind. He comes on earth unarmed. His brain is his only weapon. Animals obtain food by force. Man has no claws, no fangs, no horns, no great strength of muscle. He must plant his food or hunt it. To plant, he needs a process of thought, To hunt, he needs weapons, and to make weapons—a process of thought. From this simplest necessity to the highest religious abstraction, from the wheel to the skyscraper, everything we are and everything we have comes from a single attribute of man—the function of his reasoning mind.[6]

Man needs knowledge in order to survive, and reason is his tool of knowledge. Ayn Rand's definition of reason is: "the faculty that identifies and integrates the material provided by man's senses."[7] It is a faculty for grasping the world in conceptual terms, establishing principles, building scientific knowledge, and applying it to the tasks of understanding the world around one and living successfully in it.

Human beings cannot survive by mere percepts, or by "instincts". Even to know which objects are edible and which are not requires a process of thought. Everything man needs beyond what the automatic functions of his body provide must be acquired by rational effort—both physical needs and psychological needs. Man is an integrated being of body and consciousness. He needs food, clothing shelter; but because he has reason, he also needs (as we will see) self-esteem, art, and love relationships. The satisfaction of the needs of his consciousness help to satisfy his physical needs; and vice-versa. Strictly, they are needs not of man's body or of his consciousness, but of *man*—the integrated being. But the satisfaction of all these needs, the achievement of all the things that sustain a human life, requires the use of reason.

The development of science and technology, especially since the Industrial Revolution, and its application to man's life, has shown the immensity of the contribution that reason can and does make to human survival. One need only compare the longevity, the state of health, and the rich enjoyment of life of people in times of history when science and technology has been absent (or throttled) or places on earth where they still are.[8]

Reason as volitional

> Man's mind is his basic tool of survival . . . . To remain alive, he must think.
>
> But to think is an act of choice. The key to . . . "human nature" . . . is the fact that *man is a being of volitional consciousness*. Reason does not work automatically; thinking is not a mechanical process; the connections of logic are not made by instinct. The function of your stomach, lungs or heart is automatic; the function of your mind is not. In any hour and issue of your life, you are free to think or to evade that effort.[9]

This is man's basic choice, his fundamental *free will*: to think or not to think. To exercise his rational faculty or not. Man's freedom of action, Ayn Rand holds, flows from his freedom to initiate a state of full commitment to understanding the world around him, defining how he should act, and acting accordingly—or to drift, reacting passively to the feelings of the moment.

Drawing on an analogy to vision, Ayn Rand calls this the choice "to focus or not". We need to understand what precisely this choice is, and why Ayn Rand considers it to be *free*.

She introduces the concept of "focus" as follows:

> Thinking requires a state of full, focused awareness. The act of focusing one's consciousness is volitional. Man can focus his mind to a full, active, purposefully directed aware-ess of reality—or he can unfocus it and let himself drift in a semiconscious daze, merely reacting to any chance stimulus of the immediate moment, at the mercy of his undirected sensory-perceptual mechanism and of any random, associa-ional connections it might happen to make.[10]

73

Let's look at some examples. Consider a student studying for an exam. His purpose is to master the material and get a good grade, and he recognizes that this requires full concentration. He can focus on his course material or he can let his mind drift, latching on to any momentarily more appealing activity, letting his knowledge that his best interest is to study float in unidentified limbo.

But the alternative of being in focus or not does not arise only in situations where sustained intellectual study is involved. It arises as well in situations of practical choice. Imagine a student with limited funds, on a tight budget. He comes upon a store window exhibiting some appealing item on sale, say a shirt that would go beautifully with some other clothes he owns. He experiences a desire to buy the shirt. But then the budget comes into awareness—perhaps clearly, in words to the effect "I can't afford this", or dimly, as just an uncomfortable feeling. He faces a basic choice. He can ignore or evade that awareness and follow what happens to be in the forefront of his mind, the desire—and buy the shirt. Or he can focus on the entire situation, both the desire and the budget, and *think it through*. He may then pass up the shirt as just too expensive or he may figure out some way to afford it, perhaps by passing up a concert he had planned to go to; either way, he follows the result of his thinking.

The *fundamental* choice in this situation is not whether to buy the shirt or not, but whether to think or not, whether "to focus [one's] mind to a full, active, purposely directed awareness of reality—or . . . [to] drift in a semi-conscious daze", ignoring or evading knowledge of factors that are relevant to one's decision.

The choice to focus or not arises also in situations in which no sustained intellectual study *or* practical choice is involved. On a day of quiet relaxation, when one is taking a walk for the purpose of enjoying one's surroundings, one can walk with that purpose quietly but clearly in focus, alert to sources of pleasure in one's environment (as well as to cars or other obstacles one needs to avoid). Or, one can drift, forgetting what one is doing or why.[11]

The common element in all these cases of focusing, to put it in colloquial terms, is knowing what one is doing. More specifically, it is being committed to a full and active awareness of the world around one and of one's own consciousness, including those of one's values that are relevant to one's present situation, and being committed to acting accordingly.[12]

Such, in essence, is the alternative of focusing or not, of thinking or not. Why does Ayn Rand hold that the choice to think (or not to think) is a free choice, and not, as determinists hold, the necessary result of antecedent factors?

Her answer is, first, that it is introspectively self-evident. Each of us is immediately aware of his power to focus his mind or to let it drift. Each of us has experienced situations such as those in the three examples we have examined, and is aware of the control he has over his own consciousness. That awareness is even reflected in everyday remarks, in reaction to unwise choices that one has made, such as: "I didn't have to do that!"—"I shouldn't have let myself do that!"—"I should have thought!"

Furthermore, Ayn Rand observes, if the actions of our consciousness were determined, then all of our beliefs would be too, and we would have no control over them. That is to say, we would have no way of knowing what factors were determining our beliefs, no way of knowing whether our beliefs were based on perceptual evidence and logic, or not. We might *believe* that the factors influencing us were rational, but *that belief too* would be determined by factors we know not what. *Only* if we have initiated a process of thought directed at reality, seeking to be guided by evidence and logic—and *only* if we know that we have done so—can we claim our beliefs constitute knowledge.

If determinism were true in regard to man's consciousness, no one would know anything. But determinism is a claim to knowledge. It is therefore self-refuting. Volition, Ayn Rand thus holds, is axiomatic. It is a precondition for all conceptual knowledge, and so a corollary of the axiom of consciousness as that axiom applies in the human case.

There is much more to say about Ayn Rand's theory of free will. A fuller discussion would address, for instance, the way "antecedent factors" may *influence*—but do not *determine*—our choices and our actions. But perhaps enough has been said for readers to begin to work out the implications of this remarkable theory for themselves. After all, if Ayn Rand is right, each of us is directly aware of its truth and of the workings of the choice to think (or not) in his own mind and life.

Reason and emotion

In our discussion of man's need of philosophy in chapter 3, we were introduced to Ayn Rand's view of the relation of reason and emotion. The thesis, just discussed, that the exercise of reason is volitional, allows us a deeper understanding of that view.

75

An emotion, according to Ayn Rand, is an automatic response to a situation based on one's perception of that situation, one's identification of it, and one's evaluation of it. The evaluation is usually performed subconsciously, but the emotional response is not possible without such an evaluation, just as it is not possible without an identification of the situation. If a professor announces a surprise quiz, the typical student, upon hearing and understanding the words, may experience some anxiety, based on an evaluation that the quiz might adversely affect his grade, something he values. Should a student not hear the words at all, or not understand them—or should he not care about his grade—he would not experience that anxiety. Should he care about his grade and evaluate himself as well prepared and likely to improve his grade on the quiz, he would experience a positive emotion.

Emotions, according to Ayn Rand, are a function of one's value-premises.[13] But one's premises are formed as the result of the thinking that one has done or has not done in response to the situations one encounters through life.[14] And whether one has done such thinking or not is ultimately a matter of one's choice. Man fundamentally creates his own character, by his own choices. He is "a being of self-made soul."[15]

Because emotions (and desires) express conclusions reached automatically, and are based on premises which may or may not have been arrived at rationally, they are not a *substitute* for reason. To act on emotion or desire as such is to court disaster, as we saw in the discussion of our need of philosophy.

Emotions do permit lightning-like responses to situations and so facilitate action in times of danger. They may even point us to aspects of a person or situation that we have not noticed consciously, and such "gut feelings" are to be respected; but they must always be checked out consciously and rationally. Emotions are not, in Ayn Rand's words, "tools of cognition." They provide the means for the enjoyment of life, but only if one does not substitute them for reason.

Metaphysical individualism

Speaking to Dagny Taggart, in *Atlas Shrugged*, about the value of social interaction among rational individuals, philosopher Hugh Akston says: "You see, Miss Taggart, man *is* a social being, but not in the way the looters preach."[16]

The point of this remark in context is that men do find great value in interaction with each other, but only when, and because, they are each an independent, rational self-created individual. On the negative side, it is a fundamental rejection of the notion that man exists and can be understood only as part of a larger whole, a collective, "society". This notion depends on determinism. It holds that the source of man's thought and action is not himself, not his own consciousness acting independently, but "society"—the larger whole in which, supposedly, his values are instilled in him and his survival provided for him.

But on Ayn Rand's view, a man's survival depends on his mind, and the exercise of his mind is ultimately a matter of his own choice. Independent, rational individuals have much to gain from living with others—e.g., economic values from the division of labor, and the possibility of friendship and love. But these benefits depend ultimately on each individual's independent choice to think and produce, and then to trade values, material and spiritual, with others. Metaphysically, then, each man is, first and foremost, an individual in his own right.

Such, looking back over the themes of this chapter, is Ayn Rand's concept of man: a living being, whose means of survival is reason, whose reason must be exercised by choice, whose character is created ultimately by his choice to exercise his reason or not—a being, that is, of self-made soul. How, we may now ask, should such a being *live*? That is the subject of the next two chapters.

Endnotes

1. "A philosophical inquiry into man is not part of the special sciences, such as psychology, history, or economics; it does not define detailed laws of human thought, feeling, or action. It is concerned only with fundamentals; hierarchically, a knowledge of such characteristics is a precondition of pursuing any specialized science." (Peikoff, *OPAR*, 187-88.)

2. It is not that insentient nature has purposes—these are available only to the higher, conscious organisms; it is that living things are structured in such a way that their actions regularly have the result of sustaining themselves in existence. See *VOS*, 6 n., pb 17 n.

3. *AS*, 1013, pb 931; *FTNI*, 147, pb 121; *VOS*, 5, pb 16.

4. For a fuller discussion, see *VOS*, 6-15, pb 17-24. In speaking of the requirements of survival, Ayn Rand is not speaking of the bare

minimum needed to stave off death, but of what is required for optimal functioning across a life span. We will return to this issue in the next chapter, in our discussion of Ayn Rand's ethical principle that man's *life* is the standard of value.

5. *VOS*, 13, pb 19.
6. 711, pb 679; *FTNI*, 91, pb 78. Ayn Rand's use of the term "religious abstraction" is not an endorsement of theistic or any other religious belief. See her discussion in the Introduction to the 25th anniversary edition of *The Fountainhead*, x-xiii, pb viii-xi.
7. *VOS*, 13; pb 22.
8. Ayn Rand viewed attacks on technology as profoundly anti-man and anti-life. For her position on this, see her essay "The Anti-Industrial Revolution", in *Return of the Primitive: The Anti-Industrial Revolution* (1999), and other essays in that collection.
9. *AS*, 1012, pb 930; *FTNI*, 146-47, pb 120.
10. *VOS*, 13, pb 22.
11. Even "drifting" may be a case of being in focus, if that is a purpose consciously chosen in the knowledge that one needs the rest and that there is nothing else that one ought to be doing. On the other extreme, one can be exerting full concentration and yet be out of focus. The ancient philosopher Thales, as the story goes, while on a walk, was so busy concentrating on the stars that he fell into a well. If so, Thales was *not* in focus! He was not aware of the entire situation, which included the fact that he was out taking a walk. Full focus would have led him, if the astronomical problem was so important, to take a seat somewhere, or lean against a tree.
12. For further discussion of Ayn Rand's concept of "focusing", see Peikoff, *OPAR*, 55-69. Peikoff discusses the relation between the primary choice to focus or not and the choice of action, and in that context he explains how, according to Ayn Rand, man's choices are both caused and free. Our discussion of causality in ch. 5 has perhaps already made clear why, in Ayn Rand's view, causality does not entail determinism. (See above pp. 44-45.)
13. And the philosophical premises that underlie one's values. (See above, p. 34, and *RM*, ch.2.)
14. What appear to be conflicts between thought and emotion are really conflicts between two thoughts. (See above, p. 48.)
15. *AS*, 1020, pb 938; *FTNI*, 160, pb 131.
16. *AS*, 747, pb 590.

9

Ethics: The Objective
Foundation

The starting point of ethics

Morality, or ethics, Ayn Rand writes, is "a code of values to guide man's choices and actions—the choices and actions that determine the purpose and the course of his life. Ethics, as a science, deals with discovering and defining such a code."[1] Ethics is a *normative* discipline; it is aimed at guiding action.[2] Since human action is goal-directed, the choices a human being must make are ultimately choices of things to be pursued, i.e., of *values*.

The concept of a *value* is thus, for Ayn Rand, the fundamental concept of ethics. To understand whether there is any reason—any metaphysical basis—for choosing one way of acting rather than another, one set of values rather than another, the first question ethical theory must ask, says Ayn Rand, is:

Why does man need a code of values?
Let me stress this. The first question is not: What particular code of values should man accept? The first question is: Does man need values at all—and why?[3]

"Value" rests on " life"

To understand why we need values, Ayn Rand asks what they are—i.e., what facts of reality give rise to the concept of *value*.[4]
She answers as follows:

> "Value" is that which one acts to gain and/or keep. The concept "value"' is not a primary; it presupposes an answer to the question: of value to *whom* and for *what*? It presupposes an entity capable of acting to achieve a goal in the face of an alternative. Where no alternative exists, no goals and no values are possible.[5]

A *value*, we will agree, is not just a wish. For something to be of value to someone, he must be prepared, under appropriate conditions, to *act* for it (or if he already possesses it, to act, when necessary, to retain or preserve it.) A value is the object of goal-directed action.

But goal-directed action presupposes an entity capable of that action, and the value is a value *to that entity*. That's the "to *whom*".

Finally, for something to be a value to an entity, the achievement of that goal must *make some difference to that entity*. It must "face an alternative", in the sense that, if its action achieves that goal one thing happens to it, and if it doesn't something else happens (or the initial thing fails to happen.) That's the "for *what*". The entity needn't be conscious of the alternative, but it must *face* it, in the sense that the outcome for the entity depends on *how the entity acts*.

One value may make a difference to the achievement of some further value. The "alternative" the entity faces in pursuing the first value, then, is whether it will, by its own action, achieve that further value or not. But what difference is made by the achievement of that further value? Is there, Ayn Rand asks, some *fundamental* alternative that every value-pursuer faces, to which every value makes a difference? Is there some alternative that gives rise to the fact that there is value-pursuit at all? Her answer is Yes, in a passage we have already met, which is worth quoting again, this time in full:

> There is only one fundamental alternative in the universe: existence or non-existence—and it pertains to a single class of entities: to living organisms. The existence of inanimate matter is unconditional, the existence of life is not: it depends on a specific course of action. Matter is

indestructible, it changes its forms, but it cannot cease to exist. It is only a living organism that faces a constant alternative: the issue of life or death. Life is a process of self-sustaining and self-generated action. If an organism fails in that action, it dies; its chemical elements remain, but its life goes out of existence. It is only the concept of "Life" that makes the concept of "Value" possible. It is only to a living entity that things can be good or evil.[6]

The root of the phenomenon, and the concept, of value is, thus, the conditional character of life. Values exist because living things need to act to obtain specific objects in order to survive. It is not just that an organism must be alive in order to act. It is that it must act in order to remain alive.[7]

Life is thus the end for which values exist. It is, then, a living thing's *ultimate value*, i.e., its "final goal or end to which all lesser goals are the means." This final goal or end "sets the standard by which all lesser goals are *evaluated*. An organism's life is its *standard of value*: that which furthers its life is the *good*, that which threatens it is the *evil*."[8]

The conditional character of life thus gives rise also to the concept of what an entity *should* or *ought* to do. It *should* do that which it *must* do *if* it is to continue to exist. Only the conditional character of life gives rise to the *need* to act one way rather than another, and so gives reason to act one way rather than another. As Ayn Rand sums it up, "the fact that a living entity *is*, determines what it *ought* to do."[9]

Man's life as the standard of moral value

Living things other than man act automatically to sustain their lives. Man does not. He is not born knowing how to survive, nor does he automatically pursue self-preservation. Man's basic means of survival is his conceptual faculty, reason, but the exercise of reason is volitional.

Man must choose to think. He must choose to value his life. He must choose to discover the values his life requires. He must define these values conceptually, and choose to act on them. "A code of values accepted by choice is a code of morality."[10] Man needs a moral code—a hierarchically structured and integrated set of moral values—in order to live. "Ethics," as Ayn Rand writes, "is *not* a mystic fantasy—nor a social convention—nor a dispensable, subjective luxury, to be switched or discarded in any emergency. Ethics is an *objective, metaphysical necessity of man's survival . . .*"[11]

To guide his choices—to identify what is good for him or evil— man needs a *standard* of value. Man has a nature, he is a certain type of living being, and so the fundamental requirements of survival will be the same for all men. "The standard of value of the Objectivist ethics . . . is *man's life*, or: that which is required for man's survival *qua* man. Since reason is man's basic means of survival, that which is proper to the life of a rational being is the good, that which negates, opposes, or destroys it is the evil."[12]

The requirements of survival must be gauged, Ayn Rand explains, across a lifetime. A rational being projects into the future, plans long-range, sees his life as a whole, acts for long-range goals. No benefits can be measured short-term; they must be judged according as they support and further the knowledge, commitments, skills, activities, and enjoyments that maintain a human being across a life span. As noted in the previous chapter, survival does not mean staving off death.[13]

> "Man's survival *qua* man" means the terms, methods, conditions and goals required for the survival of a rational being through the whole of his lifespan—in all those aspects of existence which are open to his choice.[14]

Reason, Purpose, Self-Esteem

What, then, does man's survival require? Ayn Rand defines three cardinal values "which, together, are the means to and the realization of one's ultimate value, one's own life."[15] They are: Reason, Purpose, Self-Esteem. To each of these values there corresponds a virtue—a mode of action necessary to achieve that value. We will discuss each of the virtues in the next chapter and that discussion will enrich our understanding of these values. But we can indicate the essential content of each of the three values now.

Man's basic means of survival is *reason*. He must value that faculty. He must act to develop it, he must incorporate it into every part of his life, he must place its judgment above all else.

Man's survival requires that he be purposeful in every aspect of his life. It requires that he define his values clearly and pursue them passionately. He must define a central productive *purpose*—his work—

by which he supports his life, and he must integrate all his other purposes to that one.

To passionately pursue his own purposes as they are defined by his own reason, a man must profoundly value himself and his mind. He must have *self-esteem*. Ayn Rand defines self-esteem as "[the] inviolate certainty that [one's] mind is competent to think and [one's] person is worthy of happiness, which means: is worthy of living."[16]

What does Ayn Rand mean by saying that these three values are not only the means to but also *the realization of* one's life? The answer lies in the fact that life is a process of self-sustaining action. The fundamental values that sustain a life will necessarily *constitute* that life. To live a life guided by reason, in which rational purposes are pursued and achieved, and in which one profoundly values one's mind and person, *is* to achieve one's life.

Life and happiness

"Happiness," Ayn Rand writes, "is that state of consciousness which proceeds from the achievement of one's values." It is "a state of "non-contradictory joy." As such, it can be achieved only if one's values are non-contradictory, i.e., only if they are all rational values that serve one's life. Otherwise, to satisfy one value is to betray another, leaving one wracked with conflict.

> The maintenance of life and the pursuit of happiness are not two separate issues. To hold one's own life as one's ultimate value, and one's own happiness as one's highest purpose are two aspects of the same achievement. Existentially, the activity of pursuing rational goals is the activity of maintaining one's life; psychologically, its result, reward and concomitant is an emotional state of happiness.[17]

In maintaining that one's own life is one's ultimate value and one's own happiness is one's highest moral purpose, Ayn Rand is advocating an ethics of self-interest. In insisting that life and happiness can be achieved only if one holds man's life as the standard of moral value and defines one's interests rationally, she is advocating an ethics of *rational self-interest*. It is worth noting that many advocates and most critics of an ethics of self-interest define a person's interests as whatever he happens to desire. Ayn Rand does not. She defines a human being's *actual* self-interest, by reference to what a human being actually *is*—viz., a living being whose means of survival is reason. And based on that, she is able to show, as we will discuss in the next chapter, that the interests of rational men do not conflict—that, in fact, there is a fundamental harmony of interests among rational men.

The choice to live and the objectivity of value

"My morality," says John Galt in *Atlas Shrugged*, "the morality of reason, is contained in a single axiom: existence exists—and in a single choice: to live. The rest proceeds from these."[18]

Similarly, in her essay, "Causality Versus Duty", Ayn Rand writes: "Life or death is man's only fundamental alternative. To live is his basic act of choice. If he chooses to live, a rational ethics will tell him what principles of action are required to implement his choice. If he does not choose to live, nature will take its course."[19]

It is in choosing to live that a man establishes his own life as his ultimate value. Once he has done so, the axiom of existence (in the form of its corollary, the law of causality) does the rest, determining what is required to achieve that ultimate value. Moral "imperatives" are thus all of them hypothetical. There are no "categorical imperatives", no unchosen duties. Morality rests on a fundamental, pre-moral choice.

But that does not render moral values subjective, i.e., inventions of consciousness, or irrational. Just as one cannot ask for proof of an axiom, but must understand that all proof rests on the self-evident fact expressed in the axiom, so one cannot ask why one should choose to live, because all "should"s rest on that choice. If one actually chooses not to live, one makes oneself a nonentity, first figuratively, then literally. The choice to live is the choice to accept reality, to accept the fact that one *is* alive. That acceptance together with the law of causality provides the factual basis for morality.

Moral values are not subjective. Neither are they intrinsic features of reality. Moral values each have a "to whom" and a "for what". They identify the relationship of the valued object to a man's life. And they are each "*an evaluation* of the facts of reality by man's consciousness according to a rational standard of value."[20] They are factual relationships, *as identified* by a volitional consciousness using a method that derives both from the facts and from the nature of that consciousness. That is to say, according to Ayn Rand, moral values are *objective*.

Having examined the foundation of the Objectivist ethics, and its fundamental values, we turn now to the virtues that support these values, and the principles governing the proper relationships between and among men.

Endnotes

1. *VOS*, 2, pb. 13. The major sources for Ayn Rand's ethical theory are Galt's speech in *Atlas Shrugged*; *The Virtue of Selfishness*, especially its initial essay, "The Objectivist Ethics" (1961); and "Causality Versus Duty" (1970), *PWNI*, ch 10.
2. *RM*, 21, pb 18.
3. *VOS*, 2, pb 14.
4. In doing so, she is applying her general method for understanding and validating any concept. See above, p. 65.
5. *VOS*, 5, pb 16.
6. *VOS*, 5, pb 16 (quoting from *AS*, 1012-13, pb 931).
7. To make the point that *only* living things face alternatives, Ayn Rand projects an "immortal, indestructible robot, an entity which moves and acts, but which cannot be affected by anything, which cannot be changed in any respect, which cannot be damaged, injured or destroyed," and argues that it could not have any *values* (*VOS*, 5-6; pb 16.) The example is developed further by Peikoff, *OPAR*, 209-11, who explains why psychological factors could not provide a basis for values apart from their relation to life.
8. *VOS*, 7, pb 17.
9. *VOS*, 8, pb 18.
10. *VOS*, 16, pb 25 (quoted from *AS* 1013, pb 932).
11. *VOS*, 16, pb 24.
12. *VOS*, 16, pb 25. "Qua" is Latin, and means here "insofar as he is".
13. Ch. 8, n. 4.
14. *VOS*, 18, pb 26.
15. *VOS*, 19-20, pb 27.
16. *AS*, 1018, pb 936, *FTNI*, *157*, pb 128.
17. The three quotations are, respectively from *VOS*, 24, pb 31 (quoted from *AS*, 1014, pb 932); 25, pb 32 (*AS*, 1022, pb 939); 25, pb 32.
18. *AS*, 1018, pb 936; *FTNI*, 156, pb 128.
19. *PWNI*, 118, pb 99.
20. *CUI*, 14, pb 22. See also Peikoff, *OPAR*, 241-48.

10

Virtue, Self and Others
(with a brief look at
Politics and Esthetics)

The virtues

The fundamental values required for man's survival are constants. Reason. Purpose. Self-Esteem. These are values which one must develop and achieve throughout one's life.

One develops and maintains these values, Ayn Rand holds, by consistent, dedicated, passionate action. If one's reason is consistently to be one's guide, one must choose to think—consistently and passionately. If one wishes to achieve rationally defined purposes, one must work for them—consistently and passionately. If one wishes to achieve authentic self-esteem, one must, in one's actions, earn one's own deepest respect—consistently and passionately. These consistent, passionate courses of action, aimed at achieving those values, are the expression of *virtues*.

"*Value*", she writes, "is that which one acts to gain and/or keep—*virtue* is the act by which one gains and/or keeps it."[1] A virtue is a policy or mode of action. But successful action must proceed from knowledge.

Thus, in her fullest account of the virtues—in Galt's speech in *Atlas Shrugged*—Ayn Rand begins the exposition of each virtue with the words "is the recognition of the fact that." In each case the fact recognized is a fact concerning the proper use of one's consciousness necessary to achieve the values required for man's survival.

Ayn Rand identifies seven virtues. In her essay, "The Objectivist Ethics", rationality, productiveness, and pride are presented as each corresponding to one of the three cardinal values—reason, purpose, and self-esteem. The remaining four virtues—independence, integrity, honesty, and justice—are presented as aspects of rationality. For ease of organization we will follow this account. (In the presentation in Galt's speech, the four virtues just named come immediately after rationality, and productiveness and pride follow them.) We will find it helpful to quote extensively, from both presentations.[2]

Rationality, Productiveness, Pride

Rationality, Ayn Rand begins, "is the recognition of the fact that existence exists, that nothing can alter the truth and nothing can take precedence over that act of perceiving it, which is thinking." It is the "acceptance of reason as one's only source of knowledge, one's only judge of values and one's only guide to action. It means one's total commitment to a state of full, conscious awareness, to the maintenance of a full mental focus in all issues, in all choices, in all of one's waking hours." One accepts no substitute for reason, neither feeling nor "faith" nor any other alleged short-cut to knowledge.

Rationality is man's basic virtue. "And his basic vice, the source of all his evils is . . . the act of blanking out, the willful suspension of one's consciousness, the refusal to think." This is the act of evasion, of unfocusing one's mind. It is the essence of irrationality, and the source of all acts of destruction.

Productiveness "is your acceptance of morality, your recognition of the fact that you choose to live—that productive work is the process by which man's consciousness controls his existence, a constant process of acquiring knowledge and shaping matter to fit one's purpose, of translating an idea into physical form, of remaking the earth in the image of one's values."

Productive work "calls upon the highest attributes of [man's] character: his creative ability, his ambitiousness, his self-assertiveness, his refusal to bear uncontested disasters." Productiveness, as we have discussed, extends beyond productive work, which is its center, to an overall purposefulness. This is a commitment to form and identify rational values in all areas of one's life—including work, love, art, recreation, and the building of one's character (which we will discuss next)—and to pursue them with a passionate, focused intensity.

87

Pride "is the recognition of the fact that you are your own highest value and, like all of man's values, it has to be earned—that of any achievements open to you, the one that makes all others possible is the creation of your own character—that your character, your actions, your desires, your emotions are the products of the premises held by your mind—that as man must produce the physical values he needs to sustain his life, so he must acquire the values of character that make his life worth sustaining—that as man is a being of self-made wealth, so he is a being of self-made soul."

"The virtue of Pride can best be described by the term: 'moral ambitiousness'." It is the commitment to the highest rational standards for oneself. Pride is, in Aristotle's words, "the crown of the virtues"— it carries a commitment to the fullest practice of all the other virtues. And it includes a proud rejection of any doctrine calling for the sacrifice of one's mind or one's values to any alleged "higher good".

Independence, Integrity, Honesty, Justice

Independence "is the recognition of the fact that yours is the responsibility of judgment and nothing can help you to escape it . . ." It is the commitment to think for oneself, and to live by the work of one's own mind. Independence of thought and independence in action. In one's interaction with others, one produces or creates value, and then trades values with others. This applies both in the material and in the spiritual realm, in friendship and love (on which see below). The fundamental contribution independence makes to human survival is dramatized with great power in every line of *The Fountainhead*, especially in the moral character and life of Howard Roark.[3]

Integrity "is the recognition of the fact that you cannot fake your consciousness . . .—that man is an indivisible entity, an integrated unit of two attributes: of matter and consciousness, and that he may permit no breach between body and mind, between action and thought, between his life and his convictions . . ." It means that one must act on one's convictions, never sacrificing them "to the opinions or wishes of others." The fact at the basis of this virtue is the metaphysical thesis, discussed in ch. 5, of the fundamental harmony of mind and body.

Honesty "is the recognition of the fact that the unreal is unreal and can have no value, that neither love nor fame nor cash is a value if obtained by fraud—that an attempt to gain a value by deceiving the mind of others is an act of raising your victims to a position higher than reality, where you become a pawn of their blindness, a slave of their non-thinking and their evasions, while their intelligence, their rationality, their perceptiveness become the enemies you have to dread and flee . . ." Honesty, for Ayn Rand, is a profoundly *selfish* virtue, which keeps you in full contact with reality, allows you control over your existence, and allows you to benefit from the rationality of others, rather than setting it and them against you.

Justice "is the recognition of the fact that you cannot fake the character of men as you cannot fake the character of nature, that you must judge all men as conscientiously as you judge inanimate objects, with the same respect for truth, with the same incorruptible vision, by as pure and as *rational* a process of identification—that every man must be judged for what he *is* and treated accordingly . . ." Justice, too, is a profoundly selfish virtue: in rewarding the good in others and penalizing the evil, one fosters a world in which the men of rationality, productiveness and justice—whose own selfish actions further your life—thrive, and in which the irrational and destructive are thwarted.

There is a wealth more to say about Ayn Rand's view of each of these virtues and their application to the full range of situations and circumstances in life.[4]   The place to start, for further study, is with the heroes in Ayn Rand's novels, particularly *Atlas Shrugged* and *The Fountainhead*. Their lives and actions are powerful concretizations of each of these virtues.

The harmony of rational interests

We have already observed that if a man's "interests" are defined in the standard way as the satisfaction of whatever desires he happens to have, then conflicts within a man and, we may now add, between men are inevitable. Much contemporary moral philosophy, in fact, takes the existence of conflicts of interest between men as an axiom and attempts to build a moral theory on that premise. Ayn Rand rejects the notion of "interests" on which such theories rest.

Her approach, as we have seen, is to define man's *actual* interests by reference to his nature as a living being whose means of survival is his reason. It is in man's *interest* to live. It is in his *interest* to be rational, productive, self-valuing; it is in his *interest* to be independent, to have integrity, to be honest, and to be just. It is in his *interest* to trade value for value with others and not in his interest to gain values from others through deception or the use of physical force. It is in his *interest* to base his interests on reality and not see his interests as requiring that he gets whatever he wishes regardless of circumstances. It is in his *interest* to hold the context of the benefits he receives from living in a society in which other men are free to pursue their own self-interest and not to claim that it is a sacrifice of his interests if another human being is not voluntarily willing to give him something he would like, be it a job or love or anything else. The interests of rational men do *not* conflict.[5]

Love and sex

Love is the expression of one's values, the greatest reward you can earn for the moral qualities you have achieved in your character and person, the emotional price paid by one man for the joy he receives from the virtues of another.[6]

Love is a response to values. It is with a person's sense of life that one falls in love—with that essential sum, that fundamental stand or way of facing existence, which is the essence of a personality. One falls in love with the embodiment of the values that formed a person's character, which are reflected in his widest goals or smallest gestures, which create the *style* of his soul—the individual style of a unique, unrepeatable, irreplaceable consciousness. It is one's own sense of life that acts as the selector, and responds to what it recognizes as one's own basic values in the person of another. It is not a matter of professed convictions (though these are not irrelevant); it is a matter of much more profound, conscious *and subconscious* harmony.[7]

Ayn Rand viewed work and the person one loves as the two existential values of greatest importance in a rational man's life, and the greatest sources of happiness. But one cannot put love first. Love is possible only to self-sufficient individuals of developed character and self-esteem—rational, productive, proud individuals.

Sex is the most intense pleasure possible to man, when it unites the material and spiritual aspects of rational, self-valuing individuals. It is thus a central component of man's happiness. It is a form of celebration—of oneself, of the partner one loves, and of life. But that experience is possible only to those who have something to celebrate. Many people "[try] to gain self-esteem from sexual adventures—which can't be done, because sex is not the cause, but an effect and an expression of a man's sense of his own value."[8]

Politics: a brief look

Let us, in the available space, just indicate the central theses and main line of argument of Ayn Rand's political philosophy. The argument starts from a moral principle that so far has been mentioned only in passing—the evil of initiating physical force against others.

This principle is grounded in the fact that man's means of survival is reason and that the initiation of force stultifies reason. The man who abandons an independent reliance on his own reason in favor of using force on others depends on their rationality, yet he acts to harm and destroy it and them. Force is destructive both of the victim and of the force's initiator. The basic political principle of Ayn Rand's politics, then, is that no man may initiate the use of force against others. All human relations must be voluntary, based on trade (of both material and spiritual values) for mutual benefit.

The principle that no one may initiate the use of force entails that each man should be free to take the actions he judges his survival requires. This principle is the basis for the existence of *individual rights*. "A right," says Ayn Rand, "is a moral principle defining and sanctioning a man's freedom of action in a social context." Rights are "conditions of existence required by man's nature for his proper survival." The fundamental right is the right to life, which is the source of all other rights, including the rights to liberty, property, and the pursuit of happiness. The right to property is crucial. If a man has no right to keep the product of his efforts, then he is not able to sustain his life.

"A government," says Ayn Rand, "is an institution that has the exclusive power to *enforce* certain rules of social conduct in a given geographical area." The sole purpose of government is to protect men's rights, by protecting men against force or fraud. *"A government is the means of placing the retaliatory use of force under objective control—i.e.,* under objectively defined laws."

There are no "economic rights". There should be a total separation of state and economics for the same reasons that there is (or should be) a separation of state and church.

It follows from all of the above that the only proper social system is one that protects individual rights, including property rights, in which all property is privately owned—that is, *laissez-faire capitalism*.

Capitalism is not only the most productive social system; it is the only *moral* social system. It is, in fact, an unknown *ideal.*[9]

Esthetics: a brief look

Man's need of art, Ayn Rand maintains, is a consequence of the fact that his cognitive faculty is *conceptual.* To live man must acquire a vast body of abstract knowledge, including, as we have seen, *philosophical* knowledge. He must acquire a systematic understanding of the nature of the universe in which he lives, and of his own nature, including his means of knowledge. To decide how to live, a man needs to know whether he lives in a knowable universe or not; whether things happen by understandable natural law or by chance; whether he has *choice* over the course of his life or not; and whether happiness is possible in the world given what he understands it to be. The answers to such questions serve as the bridge between metaphysics and ethics, and Ayn Rand calls these answers *metaphysical value-judgments.*

But this is an enormous body of abstract knowledge, and no one can hold it all in mind, in conceptual form, at one time. Art, says Ayn Rand, enables man to hold his metaphysical value-judgments in a single sum *by bringing them to the perceptual level.* "Art", she defines, "is a selective re-creation of reality according to an artist's metaphysical value-judgments." It is "a concretization of metaphysics."

Each work of art projects, by the means of its particular medium, the artist's view of the world and of man's possibilities in it. Each viewer (reader, listener) responds in accordance with his own view. The creation and the response do not originate at the conscious level. A person's view of the world and of his possibilities in it are held in the emotional form of a *sense of life.* The artist creates from his sense of life and the viewer (reader, listener) responds from his. The enterprise remains a rational one, since one's sense of life is the product of one's philosophic conclusions (as all emotions are), and because artistic creation and response are not "mysteries" but amenable to rational understanding.

The need which art serves sets the parameters for what objectively counts as "art" or not. Works of a type that do not and cannot express metaphysical value-judgments—non-objective smears or word-salads, for example—are *not* art. This need also provides the basis for *evaluating* art. A work may present its view of the world with great power, subtlety, and integration, or it may not. One *judges esthetically* based on the artist's effectiveness in using his medium to express his sense of life. One may disagree with the content of a work of art, but admire the brilliance with which it was executed. One's highest esthetic response, however, will be to works that are both great as art and express, in their medium and by means of that greatness, deep philosophical truths.

The foregoing is a brief summary of the heart of Ayn Rand's esthetic theory. In her remarkable work, *The Romantic Manifesto*, where this theory is expounded, she presents as well original and fascinating views on: the means by which each of the different art forms communicate metaphysical content, the essential attributes of each art form (with special attention to literature), and the powerful contribution art can make to a human being's moral development. She offers a new definition of romanticism, based on its implicit or explicit acceptance of man's free will (the essential, she argues, that explains all the other characteristics of romantic art). She illustrates her discussion throughout with analyses of particular novels, paintings and musical pieces, and closes with the first printing of a short story she wrote in 1940 that dramatically illustrates the nature of the creative process.[10]

Endnotes

1. *VOS*, 19, pb 27.
2. The virtues are presented in *AS* on pp. 1018-21, pb 936-38, *FTNI*, 157-61, pb 128-31; and in *VOS* on pp. 20-22, pb 28-30. In each case the opening of the *AS* presentation will be quoted first. References will not be given for each quotation; readers will find it easy to locate them in the pages just mentioned.
3. See above, pp. 15-17.
4. See the full discussion in Peikoff, *OPAR*, ch. 7, 220-29 and ch. 8.
5. In this paragraph, I have summarized the argument of *VOS*, ch. 4.
6. *AS*, 1034, pb 950; *FTNI*, 182, pb 147.
7. *RM*, 41, pb 32.
8. See *AS*, 489-92, pb 455-57; *FTNI* 117-21, 98-101; and *AS*, 251-52, pb 236-37.
9. Ayn Rand's politics is presented in *AS*, *VOS*, and *CUI*. (The quotations in this section are from VOS, chs. 12 and 14.)
10. All the quotations in this section are from *RM*, ch. 1. The short story is titled "The Simplest Thing in the World."

11

The Benevolent Universe Premise and The Heroic View of Man

The benevolent universe premise

Two hallmarks of Ayn Rand's philosophic vision, I stated in the Introduction, are *the benevolent universe premise* and a *heroic view of man*. Now that we have surveyed her philosophic system, we are in a position to understand more fully the meaning of these theses and the basis of their profound truth.

The benevolent universe premise is the view that the universe is open to man's achievement and success—that the achievement of values and the enjoyment of happiness are the natural state, the norm, the to-be-expected. It is the view that suffering and tragedy are the accidental, "to be fought and thrown aside, not to be accepted as part of one's soul and as a permanent scar across one's view of existence."[1]

The benevolent universe premise is a metaphysical thesis. More precisely, it is what Ayn Rand calls, as we saw at the close of the previous chapter, a *metaphysical value-judgment*. It is a view of the nature of the universe from the standpoint of man's ability to achieve his ends and realize happiness.

Metaphysical value-judgments serve as a bridge between metaphysics and ethics. By identifying what is the norm, the to-be-expected, they shape a person's values, desires and ambition.

If you are convinced that great efforts are doomed to failure; that your "dreams" are meant to remain *in* your dreams; that becoming the sort of person you would like to be is also just a dream—then you will not pursue these goals (and they will remain only dreams).

If you are convinced that great things are possible; that life can be an exciting adventure in which demanding efforts pay off; that you can become a person you are proud of being—then you will be free to pursue these goals, and you can expect to reach them and achieve your happiness.

Ayn Rand recognizes that success and happiness are not guaranteed, even to a rational, moral man. Success may depend in part on choices made by others. But the profound pleasure of being a person fit for reality is always an undercurrent. Also, accidents do happen and tragedies can occur. But they *are* the accidental, not the norm, even if the loss is great. One fights the pain or accepts it, as appropriate, but one does not let oneself forget that loss is not the norm.

Furthermore, Ayn Rand insists, the greatest amount of suffering in mankind's history has *not* been due to anything about the nature of the universe. *It has been due to the philosophies men have accepted.*

If an individual holds that the universe is fundamentally "mysterious"; if he holds that man's reason is impotent to understand anything of importance; if he holds that it is "arrogant" and "obnoxious" to "take oneself seriously"; if he persists in thinking of himself and others as "*only* human" (as if the essence of humanity were error and failure)— then is it any surprise that he will live "up" to those expectations?

If a culture believes that the world is evil and that we should sacrifice in this world in order to escape, eventually, into some "higher" one, is it any surprise that the people in that culture experience a miserable, Dark Ages-type of existence?

If a society accepts a political doctrine that enslaves individuals to some "higher social good" (be it the "proletariat" or the "master race" or the "needy"), is it any surprise that society-wide suffering ensues?

The universe is not itself literally "benevolent"—it is not a conscious entity that feels anything about man. But it *is* open to man. It is, says Ayn Rand, *such that* man can succeed in it and achieve his happiness—*if* he understands the universe's nature and his own; *if* he defines objective, rational values; and *if* he chooses to pursue them with passionate intensity. To succeed in reality, she holds, man need only choose to focus his awareness on it, choose to live in it, choose to value his life in it—and work to understand it correctly, by forming and validating a proper philosophy.

We can see now the main theses of Ayn Rand's philosophic system on which her passionate advocacy of the benevolent universe premise rests.

• The world *exists*—with *identity*. A is A, and things act in orderly ways. There is nothing "mysterious" or "unknowable" about them.

• Man's conceptual faculty—which identifies and integrates the material provided by his senses—is a *powerful* faculty, able to understand *what* things are and *why* they act as they do. Man is thereby able to discover how to transform the world in such a way as to serve his needs and values.

• Man's nature is not fundamentally irrational nor is it at war with itself. Man is a unity of matter and consciousness, whose emotions are the product of his mind, so that when he brings his premises into consistency with each other and with reality, then his mind, emotions, and desires will be in full harmony.

• Man's *life* is the standard of moral value—his life *in the world*, the one reality there is. Since the purpose of ethics is to discover what values man's life requires, morality is no longer the enemy of success. There is no dichotomy between the *moral* and the *practical*—since "moral" is defined in terms of the requirements of life, and "practical" is defined in terms of a lifetime.

• The only proper political system is one that creates the conditions of freedom necessary for man to pursue his life and happiness.

The universe *is* open to man, Ayn Rand concludes, if he defines a rational philosophy and commits himself to seek his highest potential as a rational living being.

The heroic view of man

In her introduction to the 25th anniversary edition of *The Fountainhead*, Ayn Rand describes this commitment to one's highest potential, understood as she understands it, as something *reverent* and *sacred*, and the human potential as something to *worship*. She explains that these terms belong in a rational philosophy, because they capture a man's dedication to a moral ideal. They apply to the *heroic* in man.

"Heroism" is not a perspective a heroic person would take on himself. He seeks only to live up to the best possible. But the term refers, from outside, to that person's success in *exemplifying* a moral ideal. The term designates the "exceptional", but this need not be a statistical exception. A rational ideal is the exceptional only as measured against all other possibilities taken together. As a rational ideal, Ayn Rand's vision of moral greatness is open to everyone.

The same elements of Ayn Rand's philosophy on which the benevolent universe premise rests are the ones on which her heroic view of man rests. The two theses we have been discussing are, in fact, two aspects of an undivided whole that flows logically from the fundamentals of her system.

I have observed—to speak now in my own voice—that good people sometimes fail to reach the view of the universe and of human possibility that we have been discussing, because, on the issue of life's possibilities, they have insufficient trust in their own judgment and their own souls. They base their view of what's possible—in the building of one's character, in love relationships, in life in general—on what they see in the people around them, and not on what they see in their own souls as possible to man and to themselves. As a result, they miss out on so much in life. With this issue in mind, and for all my readers, I would like to conclude with lines from the end of John Galt's speech in *Atlas Shrugged*, where Ayn Rand, too, is speaking to us all.

> . . . Do not lose your knowledge that man's proper estate is an upright posture, an intransigent mind and a step that travels unlimited roads. Do not let your fire go out, spark by irreplaceable spark, in the hopeless swamps of the approximate, the not-quite, the not-yet, the not-at-all. Do not let the hero in your soul perish, in lonely frustration for the life you deserved, but have never been able to reach. Check your road and the nature of your battle. The world you desired can be won, it exists, it is real, it is possible, it's yours.
>
> . . . Fight for the value of your person. Fight for the virtue of your pride. Fight for the essence of that which is man: for his sovereign rational mind. Fight with the radiant certainty and the absolute rectitude of knowing that yours is the Morality of Life and that yours is the battle for any achievement, any value, any grandeur, any goodness, any joy that has ever existed on this earth.[2]

Endnotes

1. *AS,* 959-60, pb 883.
2. *AS*, 1069, pb 983-84; *FTNI*, 241-42, pb 191-92.

Bibliography

Works are grouped by type or genre and then chronologically by the year of first publication. (In the case of previously unpublished early writings, journals, letters, marginalia, and lecture course transcripts, the years during which the contents were written or delivered are given first.)

The first appearances of a book in each form—hard-cover, full-size soft-cover (abbrev. "sc"), and paperback ("pb")—are listed. Where subsequent soft-cover or paperback editions contain added material, both the first and the expanded editions are given.

In some cases a work was issued *only* in a soft-cover or paperback edition. In one case the paperback edition appeared first, before the hard-cover edition.

A list of abbreviations used in the endnotes appears at the end.

Early Writings

1925   *Russian Writings on Hollywood*, ed. Michael S. Berliner
                  (sc Ayn Rand Institute Press, 1999)
1926-39   *The Early Ayn Rand*, ed. Leonard Peikoff (NAL Books, 1984;
                  pb Signet, 1986)
1933   *Night of January 16th* (World, 1968; pb Signet 1971)

Novels

1936   *We the Living* (Macmillan., 1936; rev. Random House 1959;
                  pb Signet, 1960; 60th anniv. edn., Dutton 1995; pb Signet,
                  1995)
1938   *Anthem* (Cassell, 1938; rev. pb Pamphleteers, 1946; Caxton, 1953;
                  pb Signet, 1961; 50th anniv. edn. [with facsimile of corr.
                  1938 edn.], Dutton 1995, pb Signet, 1995)
1943   *The Fountainhead* (Bobbs-Merrill, 1943; 25th anniv. edn., with
                  intro., 1968; pb Signet, 1952; 50th anniv. edn., Dutton,
                  1993; pb Signet 1993; sc Plume, 1994)
1957   *Atlas Shrugged* (Random House, 1957; pb Signet, 1959; 35th
                  anniv. edn., Dutton, 1992; pb Signet, 1992; sc Plume,
                  1999)

Philosophical and Cultural Writings

1961   *For the New Intellectual* (Random House, 1961; pb Signet, 1963)
1963   *The Virtue of Selfishness: A New Concept of Egoism* (pb Signet, 1963; NAL, 1964)
1966   *Capitalism: The Unknown Ideal* (NAL, 1966; expanded pb Signet, 1967)
1967   *Introduction to Objectivist Epistemology* (pb The Objectivist, 1967; pb Mentor, 1979; expanded 2nd edn., ed. Harry Binswanger and Leonard Peikoff, NAL, 1990; sc Meridian, 1990)
1969   *The Romantic Manifesto: A Philosophy of Literature* (World, 1969; pb Signet, 1971; rev. [expanded] edn. pb 1975)
1971   *The New Left: The Anti-Industrial Revolution* (pb Signet, 1971; rev. [expanded] edn. pb 1975; repr. w/ addtl. essays as *Return of the Primitive: The Anti-Industrial Revolution*, ed. Peter Schwartz, sc Meridian, 1999)
1982   *Philosophy: Who Needs It*, ed. Leonard Peikoff (Bobbs-Merrill, 1982; pb Signet, 1984)
1989   *The Voice of Reason: Essays in Objectivist Thought*, ed. Leonard Peikoff (NAL, 1989; pb Meridian, 1990).

Periodicals edited and written for

1962-65   *The Objectivist Newsletter* (Second Renaissance, 1991)
1966-71   *The Objectivist* (Second Renaissance, 1990)
1971-75   *The Ayn Rand Letter* (Second Renaissance, 1990)

Journals, Letters, Marginalia, Misc. Writings

1926-81   *Letters of Ayn Rand*, ed. Michael S. Berliner (Dutton, 1995; sc Plume, 1997)
1927-77   *Journals of Ayn Rand*, ed. David Harriman (Dutton, 1997; sc Plume, 1999)
1944-79   *The Ayn Rand Column: A collection of her weekly newspaper articles, written for the Los Angeles Times, with additional, little-known essays*, ed. Peter Schwartz (sc Second Renaissance 1991, rev. [expanded] 2nd edn. 1998)
1945-81   *Ayn Rand's Marginalia: Her critical comments on the writings of over 20 authors*, ed. Robert Mayhew (sc Second Renaissance, 1995)
1962-63   *Why Businessmen Need Philosophy*, ed. Richard E. Ralston (sc Ayn Rand Institute Press, 1999)

Lecture Course Transcripts

1958   *The Art of Fiction: A Guide for Writers and Readers*, ed. Tore
        Boeckmann (sc Plume, 2000)
1969   *Writing Nonfiction: Its Theory and Practice*, ed. Robert Mayhew
        (sc Plume, forthcoming)

Excerpted Writings

1986   *The Ayn Rand Lexicon: Objectivism from A to Z*, ed. Harry
        Binswanger (NAL, 1986; pb Meridian 1988)
1999   *The Ayn Rand Reader*, ed. Gary Hull and Leonard Peikoff
        (sc Plume, 1999)

Exposition based on extensive discussions with Ayn Rand and on a lecture course endorsed by her

1991   Leonard Peikoff, *Objectivism: The Philosophy of Ayn Rand*
        (Dutton, 1991; sc Meridian, 1993)

Abbreviations Used in Endnotes

AS	*Atlas Shrugged*
CUI	*Capitalism: The Unknown Ideal*
FTNI	*For the New Intellectual: The Philosophy of Ayn Rand*
ITOE	*Introduction to Objectivist Epistemology*
OPAR	*Objectivism: The Philosophy of Ayn Rand*
PWNI	*Philosophy: Who Needs It*
RM	*The Romantic Manifesto: A Philosophy of Literature*
VOS	*The Virtue of Selfishness: A New Concept of Egoism*
VOR	*The Voice of Reason: Essays in Objectivist Thought*